D0122719

My Angels Wear Fur

MY ANGELS
WEAR FUR

*Animals I Rescued
And Their Stories of Unconditional Love*

DEVON O'DAY

RUTLEDGE HILL PRESS™
Nashville, Tennessee

A Division of Thomas Nelson, Inc.

TABLE OF CONTENTS

CONTENTS

PREFACE

Some people read the Bible and get amazing insight. Some people go fishing and get close to God. I have found that God has sent animals to help me understand His plan for me. When I won't listen to Him, when I can't hear Him, He inevitably sends me an "angel in fur" to show me His divine teachings.

Kindness, unconditional love, faith, hope, steadfastness, courage—all have been exhibited by the animals that have crossed my life's path. God is constant in His teachings, and He won't give up on us. Sometimes, for all of us, He has to find the key or the method to bring us understanding. For me, it has come dressed in fur, smelling of hay, or begging for dog biscuits.

If we can all be as good as the simple creatures we've been given dominion over, our lives will be rich.

> May you find joy in your days,
> May you find satisfaction in your tasks,
> May you find contentment in yourself,
> And may you find comfort in your loss.

As you cuddle up with your "angel in fur," listen to the words God might be telling you through this animal!

ACKNOWLEDGMENTS

Thank you,

Steve Bard and Lara Turner, who give all they have and all they are in the unselfish saving of animals.

The Tennessee Farmer's Co-Op, for helping with the Pet Hotline and for providing great products and good prices.

Sonya Velez, for your angel work with nashvillepetfinders.com.

Cathy Pelletier, for practicing what you preach, for continuing to consider me a writer, and for giving me Earl.

The crew of volunteers of Saddle-Up and Angel Heart Farms.

Hoyte and Jane Eakes, for everything!

Dr. John McCormick, Dr. Linda Taylor, and all the crew at McCormick Animal Clinic in Nashville.

Cherry at Nashville Humane Association.

James and Jim, for taking care of my babies when no one was looking.

Vernell Hackett, The Kinleys, Lorrie Morgan, Drew Womack, Phran Gallante, and all the Music Row "insiders" who help so much in the fight to save animals and give them a safe place to "be."

JuRo Stables, for helping me out.

Cheatham County Animal Hospital, Hermitage Animal Clinic, and The Pet Emergency Clinic on Eighth Avenue.

Helen, at Springfield Animal Control.

Judy Ladabouche, for doing such a thankless job and creating a wonderful facility!

Alisa, Jenn, Charlotte, the guy backstage at the Billy Gilman concert, Carroll, and everyone who has given my babies a home!

To the amazing pet lovers in publishers' clothing at Rutledge Hill Press: Bryan, Geoff, Larry, and precious Sara, who just plain "gets it."

The Tennessee Walking Horse Breeders and Exhibitors Association. Tracy, Bob, and Bill are among the most noble horse people I know.

Dr. Chris Shue, Debbie, and the compassionate staff at Kingston Springs Veterinary Hospital. You were an incredible, compassionate anchor in one of my most difficult moments.

Gerry House, for your friendship, support, and belief. Part of accomplishing anything is having a safe place to fall.

Al, Duncan, and Mike, for always letting me see your hearts.

Marla, Leeanne, and the amazing e-mail group!

To Steve Earle, for inspiration.

And most important, the greatest of thanks to Pat, Charles, Faith, and Campion. Your constant belief, you spiritual roots, your love around me like wings have kept me on course, on the path, and on my way. I love you.

INTRODUCTION

Over the years, animal rescue and adoption have transformed my life over and over and over. At times I have become transfixed on being almost forty and childless, until it has occurred to me that I'm not childless at all. My children just have feathers and fur—and find me completely flawless.

Although the subtitle of this book is "Animals I Rescued," none of these stories are meant to focus on my actions when I found or rescued an animal (or when animals in need found me!). On the contrary, this is a tribute to the animals that have divinely moved in and out of my life . . . and rescued me.

To me, animals exemplify all the qualities God asks of us. They love without judgment. They always turn the other cheek. They are loyal and caring, and they see through each of us, to the hidden souls of our real beings. There is nothing but simple truth and a sense of right and good in our animal friends.

If by reading any of these stories, one person is moved to adopt a new family member from a pound or shelter, it has been worth every word. If by touching a spirit with these words, someone stops by a roadside and helps a hurt stray animal in need, this book will have been a gift of life. If by reading these words, you feel a closer bond to those furry soft faces that look up at you with such adoration each day, then my time has been well spent.

Enjoy these stories and love God's creatures.

Women and cats will do as they please, and men and dogs should relax and get used to the idea.

—*UNKNOWN*

Belshazzar's Feast

Louisiana is known for incredible food; a steeping of cross-culture that blends African, Cajun French, Native American, and Southern; and strange swamp creatures of great assortment. Rural Louisiana is not, however, known for its wonderful and humane treatment of abandoned and sheltered domestic animals.

I began doing volunteer work in college, at an animal control facility located in a flood-endangered field right behind a building marked "Mosquito Control." Obviously, the animals were not considered important enough for anyone to care that they were quartered near drums of the pesticide DDT (still legal at that time). This was before visiting veterinarians began to donate their time to help with medical care for the unwanted and unhealthy strays of the earth. This was not a shelter. It was a pound—the last stop, the ninth life, the end of the tracks.

Mange was rampant, as was kennel cough. Animals were wet and shaking, and food bowls were filled with rank and stinking food mixed with water and urine. This little animal facility in the forgotten part of my hometown became my new focus. I have come to realize that this was the condition of animal facilities all over the country during the years before animal activists and volunteers began to bring change about through legal battles and elbow grease.

Growing up, I never had cats. I had been bitten by one, was allergic to all of them, and was forbidden to bring one home. My rebellious college heart naturally led me directly to the cat room at the pound. I began learning about litter cleaning and cat habits. I learned about cat diseases and survival behavior. I saw cats that were feral, sick, old, flea-bitten, filled with worms, and hopeless. Then I met Belshazzar. He was a little black kitten, so small he could fit in the palm of my hand. He probably was too young to be weaned, but he'd been left at the front gate along with a litter of siblings, squirming in a burlap sack. Some were dead, but this scrawny black kitten was wet and screaming. I fell in love.

Despite knowing nothing about cats, I asked to keep him. At that time, they didn't check adoptions much, and since they thought he'd die before dawn, they said yes. My "cat college" began at that moment.

After a trip to the IGA grocery store for some cans of evaporated milk and to the toy store for a baby doll bottle, we were in business. I heated the milk a bit, then tried sticking the nipple in the kitten's mouth. He was having none of it.

I had seen mother cats around the pound aggressively clean their babies with sandpaper tongues. So I got a washcloth, moistened it with hot water, wrung it almost dry, and gave this kitten the scrubbing of his life. I gripped the wriggling package of claws and teeth by the scruff of his neck as I'd seen cat mommies do. And like a miracle of cross-species maternal instinct and feral hunger, he began sucking the little baby bottle of milk as if it were his first and last meal. We had bonded.

We moved from bottles to bowls, a difficult transition of near drowning the first couple of times. Then we began kitten chow moistened with evaporated milk, which he took to instantly. Several of my friends sang in the university's chorale, and our musical piece that year was *Belshazzar's Feast*. As we spent so much of our time trying to get this little guy to eat, we named him Belshazzar, or Shaz for short. During this time, I smuggled him in and out of dorm rooms, sorority houses, and finally to my first apartment. I had total cooperation from the Zeta Tau Alphas, my sorority sisters, who helped hide our feline contraband from maids and tattletales. One maid figured out what we were doing, so I paid her off until the end of the semester when I moved to an apartment. Black-cat blackmail was born!

My first cat, my first cat rescue, and my first "you and me against the world" experience made us fast friends, Shaz and I. He purred and "made biscuits" with a kneading motion on my chest when it was time to wake up. He loved the shower and took his bath in the water in the bottom of the shower when I had finished.

Shaz would eat anything I put in front of him, figuring that "mom" food was always good, no matter how weird it might seem.

My roommates loved him, but he was a one-woman man. He would answer when I called his name from another part of the house. He even seemed to forgive me for having him neutered on that one vet visit. I felt so bad for him that I gave him little cans of white albacore tuna for a week. So he got fat, happy, and accustomed to his spot on the bed and his nightly constitutionals. Many a lizard and field mouse lost their lives to his hunting skills. But one cold night, he didn't bring anything home.

I came home from class to a room of my friends, who sadly told me that Shaz had climbed into the engine of a car, and when it was turned on, he was caught in the fan belt.

My heart sank and my legs buckled with it. "My baby . . . dead?"

"Well, he got out and ran screaming toward the bayou grass. We've been looking for him all night," my friend John explained.

"Then he's alive somewhere!" I screamed and ran out, tears streaming, calling, "Shaz, Shaz-baby! Mommy's here."

There was no familiar cry of response. There was no black cat running to me from the brush. There was only . . . nothing. For seven days, I cried and left out food and water. Still, no sign of my Belshazzar. My vet explained that when a cat runs away to be alone as Shaz did, he probably knows that he has fatal injuries. Cats prefer to die alone. Actually most animals leave the herd or their homes when they feel their time has come.

I couldn't accept that—wouldn't. That night, to try to cheer me up, my friends ordered pizza and threw a little impromptu party, which I was totally not in the mood for. The music was loud, everyone trying hard to be jovial, but right in the middle of the din, over all the uproar, I heard a faint "meow."

I was the only one to hear it. It was weak, but it was there.

"Shaz!" I yelled as I ran to the door. My friends thought I had completely lost it at that point. But much to their surprise and my joy, standing on the doorstep was my Belshazzar. His back leg was simply hanging from his body, and he was scarred and scratched, but he was there—alive!

I wrapped him in a towel and got him to the emergency clinic. My veterinarian met me there, explaining that surgery might kill Shaz and that a leg crushed that badly would never be usable. "Besides," he told me, "he won't be able to get around to find a litter box. What are you going to do? Take him there yourself? Most people in your position would just have him put to sleep. After all, this is going to be expensive. And, he probably won't live anyway."

That was all I needed to hear. After using my rent money to repair his leg (I left that financial problem for the next month), I took Shaz home with his new cast. I treated his wounds with aloe, hydrogen peroxide, and antibiotic cream. When he seemed bothered by his itchy cast, I used a wire and an emery board to scratch under the plaster, much as I'd seen friends do with broken arms and legs.

Every night, I made him a little bowl of cream of chicken soup. Every morning and then three more times a day, I held Shaz over his litter box so he could maneuver to take care of business. Being a fastidious fellow, he would squawk afterward for me to clean his box, as the cast hindered his "cover-up" technique. He would watch me clean up and throw away anything he found unacceptable, then wait patiently for me to take him back to his spot on the bed. Six weeks later, in I walked, and there was Shaz's cast off to one side, chewed free, and Shaz grooming his completely healed leg. The doctor couldn't believe it when I told him about the recovery.

That was more than twenty years ago, and Shaz lived a long and happy life. He taught me about cats and lives and that from his meager burlap bag beginnings, he was a survivor. Shaz taught me that hopeless was only true if you believed it. I learned that people and animals can strike an amazingly strong bond that supercedes anything possible by human or animal alone. And his greatest lesson was that when you need someone, trust enough to ask for help instead of suffering alone.

So now when I see a big black cat cross my path, I don't think about how unlucky my day will be. On the contrary, I remember the day a black cat entered my life and changed it forever. Now, that's what I call luck.

Lost

Lost, a fear that grips you suddenly.
Lost, the island you find yourself marooned upon.
Lost, a longing that is unequalled.
Lost, time that passes oh so slowly.

Lost, a feeling of being totally untethered.
Lost, a surrender to the kindness of strangers.
Lost, a swirling constant of unquenched hope.
Lost, a knowing that somewhere you are looking for me.

—DEVON O'DAY

*A dog is like an eternal
Peter Pan, a child who
never grows old.*

—*AARON KATCHER*

Toby . . . or Not Toby

It was a crisp autumn morning in New York City, and I was up bright and early at a photo shoot for a catalogue. I was a model for the Ford Agency at the time, and I was in for a long day.

It was the usual buzz of activity. Coffee and makeup and hair and wardrobe—all just so America would not be deprived of the chance to see us, the full-figured brassiere models, in all our mail-order glory. My makeup artist was a tiny auburn-haired French girl named Frederique.

Today she was in tears over a dog she had found wandering the streets of the Upper East Side. He was an old, very old, red cocker spaniel. The humane societies and the ASPCA had said that old, very old dogs were simply not adoptable. He had probably, according to them, been dumped on the streets because of his need for geriatric care. Frederique told me he had terrible anxiety and would whine and cry every time she left him. She had to find him a home. Her cat was defecating in her shoes over the unhappiness of this new housemate.

Well, I felt a dog would be fine with Barney and Blue Maxine, my cats, and I figured I could use the exercise of walking a dog. So I went to Frederique's apartment and brought this bouncing senior home. His eyes were clouded with cataracts. His teeth were worn down to nubs. It was obvious he didn't hear very well, either. I fell totally, completely, in love with this freckled cocker boy.

When he looked at you with his little blind eyes, he almost smiled. But his worn-down teeth formed a crooked smirk that looked more like Elvis than a cocker spaniel. Soon I learned the trials and tribulations of being a dog owner in the Big Apple. Walking a dog with a baggie on your hand so you could avoid leaving unkind deposits for the "friendly" New Yorkers to deal with became an adventure. Toby was one of those moving squatters who left a little trail of "surprises," so he never stopped to let you clean up. No, he pulled you as you chased him, scooping with your baggie as you went.

The snow and the salt on the sidewalks made his arthritis flare up and hurt the pads of his old cracked feet, so I made him booties to wear on cold days. He hated the cool drafts of my apartment, so I cut up a Georgia University sweatshirt for him to wear. I named him Toby after the main character in the TV movie *Roots,* because both of them had been dropped into new lives where no one knew their origins. My Toby seemed uprooted from his home and family. He always seemed to be looking for someone. He seemed to be lonely for a past that the love I gave him could not make him forget. I felt that somewhere, someone was missing his or her old friend just as much as Toby was. He was just too good a pet. He was completely housetrained and so friendly. This had to be somebody's baby.

Toby did, however, whine and drool at the door whenever he was left. That was a hint that he had been left by someone before. Dogs don't usually have a fear of abandonment unless they have been abandoned. I couldn't believe anyone could have been so cruel as to dump a precious animal on the cruel streets of New York just because it was old.

I grew to love Toby more and more. When I moved from Chelsea to the Upper East Side to 72nd and Second, I took him with me. The doormen at the apartment loved him. Blind as a bat, Toby would wag his nub of a tail and pull me with his leash to the doormen for treats. I guess they related to an old blind dog put out to pasture because some of them felt a little like that themselves.

My boyfriend, Greg, helped with the walking. We made Toby special food, because he had so few teeth left. I realized why when we took him to the park to play. He kept bringing us rocks. We'd throw his ball, and he'd chase after it. But if he could find a rock or a piece of broken cement, he'd bring that to us and send us in search of his ball. My deductive reasoning told me this was how his teeth had worn down, not just from old age.

Almost a year passed. Toby, Maxine, and Barney were fast friends. I thanked God every day for Toby coming into our lives. His boundless energy kept him blindly searching for and finding Frisbees and balls in the tiny apartment. Our days were filled with Toby's adventures. His personality was bigger than his body and more youthful than his chronological years. Still, somehow I knew we were a temporary family.

One day, I came home to find Greg crying as he held Toby. "I'm so sorry, honey. If I hadn't taken Toby, this would never have happened." He sadly looked up at me. Toby began insistently throwing his own ball and chasing it. He hated it when we talked and didn't participate in his games.

"What are you talking about? What happened?" I had a sick feeling in my stomach. I thought maybe something was wrong with Toby. After all, he seemed around a hundred. But Toby looked healthy enough bouncing around us, drool to the wind.

"I was just walking him by D'Agostino's, and someone yelled

Lancelot, and Toby ran to this girl. Honey, he knew her. Honestly, he wasn't just being friendly like he is with the doormen and kids. She's the person Toby's been looking for. But I couldn't just let her have him. I had to wait for you. Here's her number, and she's waiting for your call." Greg handed me the slip of paper with a scribbled name and number.

With tears in my eyes, I called this woman who seemed to be a connection to Toby's lost past. *Maybe it's a coincidence. Maybe he just looks like her Lancelot,* I thought.

A woman answered the phone, and completely broke down when I told her who I was. Her story unfolded like a miniseries, and I began to understand how Toby came to us.

She was a young married woman who had moved from Kentucky to be with her husband. Since New York was such a culture shock from rural Kentucky, she had talked her husband into letting her bring her old buddy, Lancelot, whom she had raised from a puppy. He was fourteen years old.

"Are you sure this is really Lancelot? I mean, he was running around the streets half starved when we found him," I said accusingly.

"And just where did you 'find' him?" she asked, just as suspiciously.

Her story continued. They had gone to Central Park for a game of touch football with her husband's friends. They had tied Lancelot to the wrought-iron fence near where they were playing. After the first quarter, she looked over to find Lancelot, leash and all, gone. She knew he would never have run away, so he must have been stolen.

I began to realize that she thought, perhaps, I was the one who had stolen her pet. "I really did just give this dog a home," I told her. "The shelters would have euthanized him. He just was too precious for that to happen." I was a little defensive by now.

For a year, she had left food at the same place in Central Park. She had heard that people stole dogs for sale or ransom. But she also heard that if they were old or sick, they were just let go on the streets. All Lancelot had known were rural roads and grassy pastures of Kentucky. He had no city survival skills. There was not a day she had not continued to look, never a day she had not cried. Being a transplant in New York was bad enough. Losing her best friend was the worst thing that could have happened.

Then she gave me the final puzzle piece.

"He has this weird little game of bringing you rocks. He started it as a tiny puppy. He loves them . . . more than balls, or Frisbees, or toys."

Now I knew my Toby was her Lancelot, and it was killing me.

"I know you are probably attached to him, and you probably won't want to give him up," she said with a catch in her voice, "but you have at least given me peace. I couldn't imagine him dying alone on these streets. Thank you so much." She was starting to sob.

"Wait. You're right, we are attached to this old guy, but he has looked for you and pined for you every single day. He has loved us, yes, but he is your baby. Where do you live?"

"Really?" she asked unbelievingly.

An hour later I met her and her husband at their apartment. Lancelot was pulling me to her door with a sense of knowing that could only be explained by one thing. He was home and this was his mama.

After a tearful hello, and a tearful goodbye, we hugged a big group hug of closure. Lancelot-Toby-Lancelot had come full circle in a city that never sleeps and has very little compassion for an old dog with no home. As I walked home with Greg, we silently held hands and cried those simple tears of loss mixed with ones of happiness over doing the right thing.

Sometimes animals are yours for their whole lives, and sometimes their lives are just yours for a passing glance. Either way, you are changed forever by their presence. I'm blessed that we were touched by that sweet blind dog, even for a year. I can never look the same again at a dog wandering any city. I will always think, *this might be somebody's baby.*

I have never heard from Toby-Lancelot's parents again. It's a page in a book that has turned. A page that ended "and they lived happily ever after."

I Can Count on You

At the end of the day,
At the end of my patience,
At the end of my money,
At the end of my dreams,
At the end of my friendships,
At the end of my hope,
At the end of my health,
At the end of my success,
At the end of my rope,
At the end of my popularity,
At the end of my youth,
At the end of my life,
I can count on you, to get me started again.

—*Devon O'Day*

Anastasia Blue Maxine

In New York City I was drawn to the ASPCA, which was filled with animals of all sorts who'd been caught or surrendered from the streets of Manhattan. I visited but never adopted because my roommates would have thrown a fit. And I must tell you, I was fitfully lonely for a pet.

Most shelters will let you volunteer in many capacities. They *need* you to volunteer! But one day, no amount of practical sense could keep me in the volunteer column and out of the pet owner one. It was the day I met Anastasia Blue Maxine.

I was going about my business in the cat room, cleaning out litter boxes and clicking softly to the kitties in their cages. Contrary to the popular school of thought that cats are not loving and affectionate like dogs, I always have found cats to be particularly lonely and in need of attention. They swish their tails, mew loudly, and purr like mini-chainsaws when they want love. They climb in the middle of your newspaper, "make biscuits" on your chest, and rub against your legs. Cats, in my opinion, have gotten a raw deal in the public relations department.

There in the back of the last cage, lounging like royalty, was a cat. She was a lovely shade of purplish blue-gray, with eyes to match. If Elizabeth Taylor were a cat, she'd have been this cat. Anastasia Blue Maxine, as I called her, was a Russian blue and part of a matched set until her sister had been adopted, leaving her alone in the cage. Apparently she hadn't seemed quite as loving as her sister at adoption time, so she was left behind when her sister was taken to a plush apartment on the Upper East Side.

The letter in the adoption file said the owners of the two cat sisters had just had twin babies and couldn't keep the cats. They wanted them to go together, if possible, as the cats were so bonded to each other. However, when pets are surrendered, you pretty much give up any control over their adoption and hope they go to a good home during their allotted days. I just felt so sorry for lonely Maxine that I took her home with me that very day.

After my three roommates gave me a ration of verbiage for bringing home a cat, they finally accepted that I was not going to take her back and decided to love her, in spite of me. Anastasia Blue Maxine, so named for her royal personality and Russian background, became our little Maxine. She had a love for expensive cashmere sweaters— not for wearing, but for sleeping on. She discovered a way to open the dresser drawers and pull out cashmere, then carry the sweater to the room she wanted to nap in. No other fabric would do. She'd curl up in a ball on it, until someone came in and found her and shouted, "Maxine, *no!*" Of course, this never stopped Maxine from just doing the same thing again later.

Maxine had to have all the attention. She'd knock everything off a bureau, tip over water glasses, and turn off the television if you weren't giving her ample love. She demanded affection, as if she knew she deserved it. Upon using her litter box, she'd scream until someone immediately came and cleaned it out. She wouldn't abide one little thing remaining in that box. I told you she was like royalty.

I moved several times in New York, and Maxine always went with me. I adopted a striped orange kitten named Barney whose owner moved away and left him with me. Maxine loved Barney well enough, but she never could understand that he was actually a regular cat, which she was not. She sat outside the litter box when he soiled it and screamed until we cleaned it out for him. She constantly groomed Barney. She was horrified when he caught a mouse in the apartment and set out to eat it. No, only Fancy Feast in her little crystal bowl would do for her.

When I left New York for Nashville, I left Barney and Maxine with Greg, who was an amazing artistic soul and loved them as much as if he'd breathed life into them himself. I always had intended on coming back to get them as soon as I had a place to keep them. But in the year it took me to get settled enough to move the cats and my boyfriend to Nashville, they all had moved to Athens, Georgia, and set up housekeeping there.

Last I heard, Maxine had passed away at the ripe old age of eighteen, quietly in her sleep. Barney is now eighteen, but seeing a revival of his youth thanks to Greg's new girlfriend's golden retriever.

Life sometimes lets paths cross, then they fork again for no apparent reason. Perhaps Anastasia Blue Maxine and Bad Orange Barney were not supposed to be mine forever. Because, in the year without me, Greg found a way to make photography his livelihood. He began to use his gift with his best subjects, Anastasia Blue Maxine and Bad Orange Barney. They were the wings to his

dreams of art, because they gave him a desire to capture their per-
sonalities on film. So these two little kittens from Manhattan's
ASPCA and Long Island's North Shore Animal League ended up
together, doing exactly what they were sent to earth to do—
become an artist's muse.

I'm just grateful to have known them all.

*If there are no dogs in
Heaven, then when I die,
I want to go where they went.*

—WILL ROGERS

Sir Winston, Earl of Nash

There he was, in a cage marked BEWARE, a matted gray schnauzer with a surly disposition. My volunteer status at the humane society allowed me the inside view behind the scenes, of animals that weren't considered fit for adoption by the public. The "back room" is a shelter reality nationwide. The infirmary of sick animals, recent drop-offs, and animals deemed aggressive are exiled to this special room.

Some get well and make it to the adoption room. Some don't. The bad-tempered ones usually fall in the latter category, as was the case with my schnauzer friend. There in red letters, was the word "unadoptable." I knew what this meant. In the year I'd volunteered, I had never adopted anything. I had seen animals die, had watched on euthanasia days, and realized the future for this little gray, growling creature.

His ears were unclipped, like Tramp, from my favorite movie,

Lady and the Tramp. He was filled with attitude and seemed to call to me from behind those bars. I opened the door to the cage, warily. He jumped—right into my arms. This dog had picked me. I called him Winston and filled out his adoption papers. The girls at the shelter saw a dog-mommy connection that was so deep, so immediate, that somehow they forgot to charge me a fee to adopt this little guy. I guess they realized that vet bills would be enough for me to handle. Since he was on the euthanasia list for the next morning, probably no one would notice if he came up missing.

Turned out, Winston loved riding in the front seat of a vehicle. He was also quite particular about where and how he rode. I thought nothing about the pressure he would cause at home, however. When I walked in with Winston, my boyfriend at the time went ballistic. They hated each other from the minute they saw each other. No matter where I was in the house, Winston would be between "that guy" and me, growling in protection. He would find a way to leave "tootsie rolls" in the bathtub in defiance, right before my significant other took his shower.

Winston urinated in his shoes. He marked his side of the bed. The list went on. Apparently, Winston had figured this guy out and was going to let me know, no matter what it took. An abusive relationship that had gotten out of hand was ended and healed by a little gray schnauzer, the day the announcement, "It's either me or that dog," was made. In all the years of putting up with the pain of this man, one day and one dog gave me reason and the wherewithal to leave. That was the first time Winston saved me.

You see, I was raised with wonderful values of commitment and love. I have always known the way that is right. But, quite honestly, I am human and all humans fall short. We make mistakes and pay the consequences. Sometimes we hit a bend in the road that makes us feel unworthy of love, so we find the lowest place to hide. We punish ourselves with bad habits, bad choices, and bad relationships. I guess we forget that forgiveness and grace are always an option. Sometimes God teaches us forgiveness, compassion, and unconditional love by making us desperately need them ourselves.

My mother always told me, "Never say what you're never going to do because it's the first thing you *will* do." She was right . . . and I was wrong. I found myself in an abusive relationship, and Winston helped rescue me. Through him I felt loved again for the first time in a long time. If he loved me then I must be worth something. Somewhere in the darkest of the dark I saw a little light. I followed Winston right into a new life.

We found a place to live, in a house with friends. Winston and I walked daily, giving me the exercise I needed to drop sixty pounds. We took rides together. He went to voice-over studio sessions with me. Everywhere I went, Winston went. He was totally devoted to me. Other people would call his name, but he would never take his eyes off me. We were a duo—a team! One night in the house I shared with my roommates, Winston began angrily barking to wake me. Sleepily, I ignored him, until as a last resort he pulled all the blankets from the bed. In my blurry early morning stupor, I realized why he'd been so insistent. The house was on fire. I got the fire department called, the fire out, and the danger ended all because of a schnauzer that would not give up. That was the second time Winston saved me.

That year, I bought my first house. We added two cats, which Winston loved. He'd sit contentedly as they groomed him. The left foot of my bed was Winston's place. No matter what, anything on that spot had to be moved before bedtime—even if Winston stayed with someone else while I was out of town. He'd bark around ten in the evening and run to that spot on the bed, as if to say, *it's bedtime; get back here and get my place ready.*

For a shelter dog, he worked a lot. He did some television and print work, the most noteworthy as the schnauzer on the Oster Pet Clipper box and instructional video. He loved the spotlight, as long as I was on the other side of it.

Winston got to know the neighbors. He'd run to Mrs. Ruth's back door and scratch until she opened it and gave him a weenie (that's rural for *hot dog*). He loved visits with Mallory, the Jack Russell from down the street. He was terribly unhappy if we didn't have a "mommy and me" drive at least once a week. As the years passed, age began to show as Winston lost teeth and arthritis set in.

I made him special meals every night. I gave him natural supplements for his bones. He knew that no matter what he needed, he could come to me and somehow it would be provided.

After returning home from a trip to London, England, I realized something wasn't right about Winston. He was dazed and seemed disconnected with the world around him. I took him straight to my veterinarian, Dr. John McCormick. During that drive Winston began having seizures. I had never seen anything like it. Knowing that an animal's time is coming is one thing. . . being in that moment is another thing entirely.

We started transfusions, IVs, and anything we could do to stabilize him. Nothing helped and his liver was failing. I made the decision that you make when your best friend is in agony, and your best friend happens to be an animal. Dr. McCormick talked me into giving him one more night of drugs in hope of a miracle. I spent most of the afternoon on the floor of the vet's office talking to "my guy."

I thanked Winston for the courage he gave me to leave a bad relationship. I thanked him for keeping me company on many a lonely night. I thanked him for the rides, the walks, and the time he risked his life by jumping out my car window and chasing a state trooper onto the roof of his patrol car after he stopped me for speeding. I thanked him for his friendship.

Then I told him goodbye and gave him leave to go to that place where best dog friends go when they leave you. I went home, preparing for my next morning's task, the hardest thing I would ever do. Within minutes of my leaving the doctor's office, I got a call. Winston was gone. He had fallen asleep on his own. Even in his passing, he protected my heart in the kindest way he could in his final breath.

When we checked his records, everyone was amazed to find he was eighteen years old. Dr. McCormick said he lived so long because he just plain wanted to. Winston had found a place where he was needed, and dogs love being where they are needed.

From the "beware" and "unadoptable" sign at the shelter, Winston had proven the world wrong. He had been anything but unadoptable.

His ashes are kept on my desk, with a gold emblem that reads:

> *Goodbye sweet Winston,*
> *You have earned your wings.*
> *Fly now to heaven, and wait for me.*

I believe that animals do indeed go to Heaven and that paradise is not just a place reserved for humans. I have faith that Heaven is where our animal angels begin, where they are sent from, and where they return when their work on earth is done.

To this day, no pet I have ever owned will sleep on the left side of my bed in my Winston's favorite place. They walk around it, carefully, as if he is still there. Perhaps in some way, in the spirit way of animals and guardian angels . . . he still is.

You will always be lucky if you know how to make friends with strange cats.

— COLONIAL AMERICAN PROVERB

Mingus' Tiny Mews

The sound of a kitten in distress isn't a huge sound. It is hidden in the cadence of crickets and train whistles. It is masked by the wind and cloaked by the sounds of cars passing by. But one day, a tiny mew pierced through the night, and we found Mingus.

Mingus was a kitten that came out of nowhere and hid in the engine of my friend Ruth's car. Ruth called me and said, "I think there's a cat in my car. Can you come see if you can get him out?"

Sure enough, as we shined the flashlight under the chassis, the tiniest gray tabby with delicate blue eyes blinked in fear. He couldn't have been more than five weeks old. The adventure of trying to capture a hissing half-pound of feline fur is never easy. But a few lacerations later, Mingus was mine.

He was starving, as proven by his lapping of the concoction of evaporated milk and kitten chow I made. I named him Mingus because of the sound he made when he mewed.

"Miiiiiingus . . . Miiiiiingus," he'd say each morning as he peeked around the shower curtain. He said it each morning at the food cabinet where his kitten chow was stored. He said it *purringly* each morning when he woke me "making biscuits" on my chest.

Mingus was adopted at a farm in Franklin, Tennessee, and loved by a little girl, who, I am sure, is a teenager by now.

I think what I learned most from Mingus is the need to listen. Every day, there is a tiny sound of life that can be easily forgotten, hidden, and ignored. It's that vulnerable side of us that makes us run when we want to stay. It makes us hide when we want to be found. It makes us strike out when we want to be touched.

Perhaps the most important thing we could ever do is give ourselves a good listen. Above the din of cars and kitchens, over the noise of computers and children, between the crash of short tempers and drama—we should be still. We should listen to the faint mew of that vulnerable kitten within.

We should tune in. We should wait for God's voice. It is the voice we forget exists. It is the one we choke down. It is the voice of truth that scares us so much.

As I remember the sound of that tiny mew, I am reminded of that part of my being that desperately needs comforting. As it was given to a little kitten, may I remember to give love to myself and be aware of the other "tiny" sounds of people in need around me.

If a dog will not come to you after having looked you in the face, you should go home and examine your conscience.

—WOODROW WILSON

Sweet Magdalene

One morning one of the listeners of our radio show, the *House Foundation* on WSIX–FM (where I have been producer and token "chick" for more than fifteen years), called about a dog in her front yard. It had been thrown from a moving car and was just lying there. I was on my way the minute the radio show was over at 10:00 A.M.

I drove to the house where the young lady lived. The dog was still lying on the front lawn.

"Is it . . . dead?" she asked.

"No, she seems to be breathing," I answered as we got closer. I saw that the dog's breathing was labored and she was just skin and bones. She was gashed all over her body and covered in red mange. From the looks of the scratches and cuts, she might have been used as pit bull bait. Often fighting dogs are enticed to fight by putting passive dogs in the fight pit. The passive dog is held by its front or back paws and dipped into the pits and pulled out over and over. Sometimes it is just dropped in and chewed to bits.

If you could call a dog in this condition lucky, she was lucky. I took her immediately to the vet. They treated her cuts and mange, wormed her, and gave her shots. She stayed at my house, outside in a special dog house I made for her, quarantined away from my dogs. I handled her with rubber gloves as she healed from the mange. I wrapped her cuts with aloe plants and gauze bandaging. She healed without so much as a scar.

The malnutrition was something else entirely. Magdalene, or Maggie, as I called her, was a boxer. Her lovely fawn coat and big boxy head were a mess because of her ill-treatment. I began feeding her good nutritious food, canned and kibble.

Then one morning, I went out to hear squeaks, whines, and cries. It sounded like puppies. I opened her makeshift doghouse, and inside on the soft cushions were three of the fattest roly-poly puppies you've ever seen. One was a brindle, one black and tan like a hound dog, and one white with a pink nose that had one black speck.

In Maggie's malnourished stage, even the vet hadn't realized she was pregnant.

What was I going to do with puppies? That was a question I didn't have to answer for long, because Maggie was a wonderful mother. As she healed, her pups grew. And when it came time for weaning, I took everyone to the vet for a checkup and found homes for every single puppy in the Wal-Mart parking lot. Each new owner went home with a new puppy kit I'd put together, and Dr. McCormick has had all three puppies as patients through adulthood.

Now the story couldn't end there, because as puppies find homes, often mama dogs do not. Maggie, the sweetest dog in the world, got spayed and needed a new place to live. I could keep her as a foster, but she needed a permanent home with love.

I called on the Williamson County Animal Shelter for help, and they helped me find a home in four days. Maggie lives with a family and watches over their children like they were her own.

From her violent past to a totally loving future, Magdalene was home.

Probably the biggest person to thank in all this is a stranger whose name I never knew. She was the kind heart who called and said *please help me with this dog.* She could have ignored her conscience, and Maggie would have died there in her yard. She could have called an animal disposal service, and Maggie would have been put down somewhere. But because of someone who decided it was her responsibility to do something, four families have found the joy of unconditional love.

Every day we pass a Maggie. Sometimes it's an animal, sometimes not. Sometimes it is a mother in line at the grocery store who doesn't have enough money to buy milk. Sometimes it's an old man staring out the window of a nursing home. Maybe, if we all took responsibility to help, or ask for help, for the Maggies we see, the ripple effect of joy would be immeasurable.

Trust Me

If you are in need, you can trust me to reach out.
If you are hurting, you can trust me to soothe you.
If you are sleepy, you can trust me to allow you rest.

If you are lonely, you can trust my friendship as good and true.
If you are thirsty, you can trust that I will give you water.
If you are alone, you can trust that you won't be for long.

If you are angry, you can trust that it will pass.
If you are resentful, you can trust that letting go
    will ease the pain.
If your soul is hungry, you can trust the food of my spirit.

If you are broken, you can trust me to pick up the pieces.
If you are lost, you can trust that I'll find you.
If you are unsure, you can trust that I'll be here.

– DEVON O'DAY

If you pick up a starving dog and make him prosperous, he will not bite you. This is the principal difference between a dog and a man.

—MARK TWAIN

Chittlin'

A whimpering cry insistently called out to me one day when I was volunteering at the Nashville Metro Pound. The "pound" was the old animal control facility that is no longer being used, thanks to some amazingly diligent hearts in Animal Care Taskforce (A.C.T.) Now, a Nashville organization that includes many country music artists.

There, in a dirty, stinking cage, was a puppy with his ID collar around his middle instead of his neck. He looked to be part Chihuahua, part dachshund, part boxer, and part rat. I named him Chittlin' because that's exactly what he looked like—a chittlin', a fried southern "delicacy" (made, if you really want to know, from pig intestine). His little belly was swollen like the rat in the children's movie *Charlotte's Web*. His head was so small that it seemed to have been stuck on the wrong body, like Mr. Potato Head's hat.

When I took him out to the adoption desk, the director asked, "You wanna take *that* thing home?"

"Yes, he looks so ugly, he's cute, so I have to take him. Anyway, he's so pitiful. . . I don't think he'll last in here much longer," I answered.

So I paid my adoption fee and took him directly to the Bordeaux animal clinic. It was the closest place, and this animal needed help fast. With the shots and worming done, we headed home. His entire little stomach was just a fistful of hookworms, so the night was probably going to be long and graphic, the vet's assistant warned me. It was. I learned that the deworming process for a dog in this shape was not for the faint of heart or stomach.

As Chittlin' began to grow, he grew long like a weenie-dog first. Then his head began to develop like a Chihuahua's. The third stage was his legs, which grew longer like a boxer's. Chittlin' was honestly the funniest-looking dog I have ever seen. He was smart as a whip and retrieved anything I threw. He did commercials with me, using his "so ugly I'm cute" appeal to its full potential.

I knew when I brought Chittlin' home that he would only be a foster because I had too many animals already. So as difficult as it was, I began running ads in the animal section of the paper. After careful screening, I placed Chittlin' on what I thought was the right home for him—a farm, described in the most beautiful detail. I kissed my foundling goodbye and stood in the doorway of my house until the car had disappeared from sight.

Something began to bother me that night about the adoption and nagged at me until I drove to the address the people had given me. I just knew something wasn't right. As I pulled up, I saw doghouse after doghouse all over the yard, with dogs chained in front of each, all over the yard. Then I saw a kennel of pit bulls beside the house, and beside the house was a pit, used for dogfights. My heart sank. I had given my Chittlin' to a group who used dogs like him as "training" bait for fighting American Staffordshire terriers (the "official" name for pit bulls). With tears rolling down my face, I debated the wisdom and safety of walking to the front door and asking for my dog back.

Then I heard a whimpering yelp that could only belong to my Chittlin'. I looked around, and there at the edge on the front row of doghouses was my baby, straining to break free. I don't know what possessed me, except for the fearless faith of doing what I had to do, to run and unfasten Chittlin's collar and run like the wind to the car with him. We gunned the engine and left in a cloud of red dirt road dust.

Chittlin' looked up at me and began to lick my face in gratitude, as if to say, "I'm so glad to see you, but why on God's earth did you send me *there?*"

I learned from that moment to go to houses with a dog I'm adopting out. I learned better questions to ask. I learned that dog fighting in my county is illegal, but just across the line in other counties, regrettably it *is* legal.

I've always felt guilty about leaving the other dogs I saw chained. But at times in animal rescue, you must weigh the odds and do what you can do. I saved the one I knew I could, the one who had trusted me to find him a good home, and called the sheriff's department about the others. Animal cruelty charges are not easy to enforce, but they are easier now that people are becoming more aware of these situations.

As for Chittlin', he moved in down the street from me with a young married couple who now consider him their "only child." They saw him at my yard sale and thought he was "just so ugly he was cute"—and I knew he *had* to belong to them.

Brown

The most beautiful color in the world is brown,
At least when I'm looking into your eyes.
I find nothing but love staring back at me,
In the most comforting shade of chocolate.

Shoes that color stay home on good occasions.
A dress that color isn't in my seasonal palate.
Hair that color looks ridiculous on me.
But on you it just fits.

You say everything with those eyes.
"I neeeeeed a walk."
"I want a bite of whatever that is you're eating."
"I love you."

I get mesmerized by the comfort I find,
I am held by your devoted gaze,
I hear what you're thinking,
And I am home.

I can't believe that there was a time
When I didn't like brown . . .
And now, somehow because of you
It has become my favorite color.

— DEVON O'DAY

What dogs? These are my children, little people with fur who make my heart open a little wider.

—OPRAH WINFREY

Yogi's Gift

I have always loved the spirit of golden retrievers, yet had never had one during my adult life. So when I read the ad one morning offering a free golden to a good home, I called right away, a little before seven. Of course, I was the first call, and we made an appointment to meet midday.

As I walked in, the owner sweetly said that the phone had gone nuts after I had called, but since she had promised her Yogi to me, she felt she had to fulfill that promise, no matter the number of calls. Of course, now I felt obligated.

Obligation turned to complete and utter joy as I looked at the sliding glass door to the patio and saw this huge red shining smile of a face. When the door was opened, he ran right to me and stuck out his paw.

"He wants you to shake," his owner coaxed.

I shook, and melted into the heart of this big gentle guy.

Because of a new baby or because of children's allergies, Yogi had been exiled to the back yard. Anyone familiar with a golden would know that goldens have to be near you, or they die of a broken heart. Yogi had loved the children of the family so much, I was afraid my single life would be boring to him. I was so wrong.

I took him on vacation to Florida's St. George's Island that year. He loved running headlong and sailing into the waves head first. Toddlers would wander toward the surf, and Yogi would head them off before they hit water or grab them by their Pampers and gently hold them so their mom could get to them. One mom was so impressed, she asked if I was interested in selling Yogi to them. The answer was a quick, decisive, positive, and absolute *no*.

Yogi began to go everywhere with me. He went to radio station remote broadcasts dressed in a station jersey. He posed with children for pictures. He went to the lake for a swim with me on warm days. Then one day, I found Yogi had a unique and wonderful gift.

A friend called about using Yogi as a therapy dog for children with mental and physical challenges. Yogi had never done anything like that, but his temperament around children was so calm, I thought, *why not?*

So we dressed Yogi in his favorite bandana and had him smelling of his FreshNClean cologne as he bounded into the first school full of children.

There were wheelchairs and walkers and tail-pulling screamers of all ages. Yogi took everything in stride, and even the children who were frightened to death of dogs warmed to his presence. Judged a successful visit by all the teachers and aides at the school, we loaded up for school number two.

This second school was full of autistic children. The teachers told me to expect very little because these children were not likely to react much to outside stimuli. Well, these teachers had never witnessed Yogi's power over children. The children moved slowly to him as he sat quietly, letting them soak up his love and light. Some threw their arms around him; others pulled his ears and yelled with delight in his sweet face. Never did he growl or complain, responding to every prod and poke with a soft pant of acceptance.

One little girl, I was told, had never had any response to anything. She was trapped in her own little private world, and no one had been able to reach her. As the teachers explained to me that this child could not walk or talk and would never understand that a dog was in the room, a little miracle was happening behind me.

"Would you look at that!" one of the teacher's aides exclaimed.

There in the center of the children, curled up inside the circle of Yogi's warmth as he lay on the classroom floor, was this precious little girl. Her arms were wrapped around Yogi with her fingers woven tightly into the hair on the scruff of his neck. Her little legs were under her, making her a tiny protected ball in Yogi's cocoon.

One teacher cried. No one moved or spoke for a moment. Somewhere in this child's private world, the unspoken language of an unconditional heart had beckoned, and she answered.

Yogi is getting old now and has to be helped in and out of the truck. But he still loves children, and he still loves to do his job. He knows that when I put on his bandana and a sweatshirt, he's going to "work."

I often think about the sweet family who raised my golden angel and unselfishly gave him a new home when he was two years old and couldn't live in their home anymore. I wish they could know what an important place he has filled with some special children in this world and what a deep place he has touched in my heart. For their gift and Yogi's, I will always be eternally grateful.

For every beast of the forest is Mine, and the cattle on a thousand hills. I know all the birds of the mountains, and the wild beasts of the field are Mine.

—PSALM 50:10-11

Her Name Was Lucky

To most people, animal rescue involves neglect or cruelty and cute cuddly cats or dogs. However, as you read these stories, you will realize that *rescue* is a relative term. Sometimes, rescue simply involves filling the gap when Mother Nature falls short.

People may not think of cattle farmers as having hearts. We see pictures of cattle herded through chutes, transported in crowded trailers, and run through slaughterhouses. But being a farm girl raised around my grandfather's herd, I found a different truth than any animal rights group may show you.

My grandfather, Larry Walker, was a Southern Baptist preacher who also farmed eighty acres. He raised cotton, soybeans, row crops, and cattle. The cattle weren't a big money maker but were mostly food for his family. I hope I do not offend vegetarians by saying that he was a humane farmer. His Native American roots were never discussed, but I learned from birth a healthy respect for God's land and

God's creatures. My grandfather prayed as he plowed and he prayed as he threw out hay. He prayed over the bounty and he prayed over each animal that fed his family. He was a hunter who never took more than the family needed to survive and prayed over every meal in thanks for its provision. If this gives offense to anyone that an animal's life was taken, I apologize. But I find it necessary to explain the difference in careful custodianship of God's creatures and trophy kills or mass slaughter for profit. There *is* a difference.

PawPaw would often quote scriptures as we did farm chores. Genesis told us, he said, that we were given "dominion over the earth and its creatures." That, to my grandfather, was a huge responsibility. From the deer and the catfish, to the calves born on his farm each spring, we were given the job of taking care of them. We were not put here to rule or destroy, but to protect, care for, and use only what we need.

My grandfather and grandmother helped a lot of people with their animals because a vet cost money, and out in the country there just weren't many vets. Farmers gave their own vaccinations, delivered their own calves, and treated their herd's diseases. When an animal died, the body was burned to avoid the spread of the disease that killed them.

I can remember as a very young child being sent in to "doctor" a sore udder on a cow. Probably today it would be considered too dangerous a job for a six-year-old. But PawPaw said, "You're never too young to learn how to take care of God's critters." So he'd send me in armed with udder butter and "alkyrub" (PawPaw's word for wintergreen rubbing alcohol).

Once we got a call from a neighbor whose young steer had fallen into a tar vat. We lit out with a red gravel trail of dust behind us and helped pull this poor animal out of a place that should have been closed off. My grandfather didn't reprimand the farmer for the stupidity of leaving a tar vat open around cattle, but I could see it in his eyes and his stiffened jaw as he helped pull the calf out.

The pitch had set up, so it was impossible to remove. We tried mostly to get it cleared from his genitals, so he could urinate properly and not develop sepsis. We quickly cleared his airways and all other orifices, but it just didn't look good. That steer didn't make it, and no one could have done anything more to save him. I learned then what "dominion" over the earth meant. It meant knowing that we have been given the good sense to see around corners and try to prevent needless death and suffering of creatures that can't always watch out for themselves. Accidents happen, but there is no room for stupidity around animals.

My grandfather taught me love of animals, as did my grandmother. You may not realize that farmers often name their animals, but they do. Animal rights organizations don't always give farmers credit for loving their animals, but they do. Small-town American farmers are responsible custodians to the animals they consider both gift and livelihood.

My grandfather taught me about feeding animals, as he walked through his herd of cows calling them by name. Old Sukie was so ugly. She had eye cancer, and he showed me how to treat her affliction with blue lotion. Ben was the Hereford bull with the curly top knot and a sweet disposition. Then there was Jersey. She was a jersey dairy cow that provided milk for all of us early on, but soon became the mama of some of the best calves in the herd. She was just beautiful.

Her coat was a creamy tan, which burnished into black marking along her head and around her eyes and tail. She had loving black-brown eyes that innocently looked at you when you came to milk her. She was always the first cow I ran to when I got to PawPaw's. There is something mesmerizing about the smell of a cow's breath when they are munching on green grass. It's an organic clean wonderful smell of my youth that I miss sometimes, especially when I'm stuck on an asphalt freeway in traffic.

As PawPaw walked through the herd, the animals would come to him as if he were a magnet. He'd softly speak to each one, patting it on the head. They'd literally gather around him, and if he sat down on a stump in the pasture, it wasn't long before the cattle would sit at his feet. It was as if they knew this man would care for them.

That was important when Jersey got in trouble delivering a calf. During the spring, we always made runs in the morning and early evening to check on the pregnant cows to see if they were delivering all right. On this particular evening, Jersey was in delivery distress. After many, many, many calves delivered with ease, this baby was not going to come into the world without a struggle. My grandfather did what they call "pulling a calf" as Jersey was taking her last breath. He cleaned out the airways of the baby, and showed me how to milk out the colostrum from Jersey's dead udders.

That baby had to get the colostrum within its first few hours of life for her to have any chance at all to survive. The birth colostrum is the immune liquid of life a mother gives to her baby. As I learned about survival, I saw my grandfather had tears in his eyes. I was holding the bottle for the new baby when I realized my PawPaw knelt in prayer by Jersey, his hand on her head.

"You've been a good ol' girl, Jersey. . . and I thank you," he said, with a silent moment after.

The fire burning that day was a sad one, but tears are allowed only for a little while when you have a hungry calf without a mama around. Lucky, as we called her, learned the sound of a milk bucket. It was a galvanized bucket filled with calf replacement formula, with a long white nipple on the front. Lucky could hear the screen door slam, and she'd start bawling at the gate. We'd all take turns feeding her, and she'd eat like there was never going to be another meal.

Not only did Lucky survive, but she became my first milking experience. I learned never to put the milk bucket behind a cow's back feet when it's full. One well-placed kick would spill milk everywhere. I also learned never to put your foot behind a cow being milked if you don't want to get stepped on.

Lucky gave us years of beautiful calves and remained like a puppy when any of us went to the pasture. She followed us everywhere we went. I guess she always thought of us as "mama." She is certainly proof that God provides for "lost causes."

Now, only ghosts remain from that time at the old family farm in Jonesville, Louisiana. The big shed was blown away in a tornado, the fences lined with milk and wine lilies have long since broken down, and the cows no longer graze quietly as the sun sets along Little River. But the spirit of my grandfather still moves among the may-pop vines, and the shadows of the pecan trees. I can hear the faint *whoooo, suk suk suk* call from my grandmother Cora getting the cows to come in for the evening meal, if only in my memories. And I remember a wobbly calf named Lucky standing at the back gate crying for milk. Those sounds, that time, those memories will always be with me to keep me grounded and to remind me that we are the caretakers of God's universe—and it is the greatest of responsibilities.

A Prayer

Lord, make me an instrument of Your peace.
Where there is hatred, let me sow love.
Where there is injury, pardon,
Where there is despair, hope,
Where there is darkness, light,
and where there is sadness, joy.

O Divine Master, grant that I may
not so much seek to be consoled, as to console;
To be understood, as to understand;
To be loved, as to love;
For it is in giving that we receive . . .
It is in pardoning that we are pardoned;
And it is in dying that we are born to eternal life.

—ST. FRANCIS OF ASSISI,
PATRON SAINT OF
ANIMALS

God sat down for a moment when the dog was finished, in order to watch it . . . and to know that it was good, that nothing was lacking, that it could not have been made better.

—RAINER MARIA RILKE

Tennessee Tess

There was a scratching at the door. I opened it to find Bud, from the construction crew down the street, and a little dog by his feet. The dog ran past me, right into the house.

"She's been up the street on the site for about three days. She musta got dumped off or somethin'. We knew you'd know what to do with her. She's awful cute, ain't she?" Bud smiled, with that twinkle he often had as he talked about dogs. He did some lawn work in the neighborhood, including mine, and we often had dog conversations.

"She likes baloney sandwiches too." He smiled as he waved, walking away, explaining he had a lot of work to get back to.

Great. Another one. How did I get on the pet hotline? Did I have some kind of invisible sign that I wasn't aware of saying, "leave your animal here"?

Sitting at my feet was a perfectly groomed mixed-breed puppy about six months old. She looked like a cross between a basenji, a shrunken German shepherd, and a coyote. Her eyes were rimmed in black against a light sand-colored coat that made her look as if she were wearing eyeliner. She had a bit of a Cleopatra look about her. What struck me was how incredibly clean she was. Strays on the streets normally looked bedraggled and dirty, but not this gal. She was prissy and clean as a whistle. She sat looking at me as if this were her house, as if to ask, "now what?"

Sometimes animals enter your life that you know will be transients. This was definitely one of those. I simply had no room for another dog, no matter how beautiful she was. My mom flipped when I told her just before her Christmas visit there was a new dog in the house.

"You *cannot* have another dog! Where will you put her?" my mother asked.

"Probably in the guest room with you when you come up for Christmas," I answered smartly.

The vet clinic loved her. She was spayed and vaccinated within the month, but I still had no perfect adoptive parents for her.

Nightly, I was reprimanded by my parents about finding a home for Tess before the holiday. In animal placement of strays, I have found the holidays to be the absolute most impossible time to find homes for anything. Everyone is traveling, and no one wants to have a new pet to worry about. I had a feeling this dog might indeed be spending the night in the guest room with my mother and father during their holiday visit.

The Christmas holiday came, as did my parents, and, yes, they did spend the night with the new dog. But much to my surprise, when it came time to drive back home from Nashville to Louisiana, the new dog was in the back seat of my parents' car.

"She's just so cute, and smart, and . . . clean!" my mother said. "I've always wanted a little dog like that!"

No one was more surprised than I when I watched them drive away. Two little mascara-rimmed eyes peered through the back windshield as they left. For some reason, I didn't feel this was the last stop for the unnamed transient that had spent the holiday with us.

My sister, Faith Ford, who is an actress, had left Hollywood for a post-holiday trip to Louisiana a few days before going back to work on her TV show. She and her husband usually spent New Year's in Louisiana to avoid the hustle and bustle of the city during the changing of the year.

A few days later, I got a call from my mother, who said our little transient dog was no longer at her house. She was on a jet to Los Angeles. It had been love at first sight between her and my sister, Faith. My mother told me she also had a name—Tess. She's Tennessee Tess.

Tess adjusted to the Los Angeles lifestyle right away. She sat poolside and hiked canyons. She had an uncanny knack for predicting earthquakes, which came in handy in California. Tess had never been a particularly gregarious little dog, but she bonded with Faith as if an invisible cord connected them. In need of protection, Tess took Faith as her new ward. Tess never took her eyes off of Faith as she bustled about the house.

Tess was a long way from the puppy begging baloney sandwiches at that construction site in Tennessee. She had to travel quite a distance to find her best friend. Now, as I look back at the bond between my sister and this foundling, I am struck with how many impossibilities are marked off the statistic chart when a perfect match is made between animal and human.

Since that day, Tess has been in magazines and in books about celebrities and their pets, and has greeted many a "star" in those Hollywood Hills. But she's never let fame go to her head. No, Tess just accepts all the hoopla as one of life's compromises when "your human" is in show business.

Turns out, Tess entered Faith's life just in time to ride the current of life's traumatic waves and be her helpmate and friend. When that love connection happens to anyone in life, I don't think it's ever a coincidence. On the contrary, I believe God has a way of sending us unconditional love, even if it's in animal form . . . at the very time He knows we'll need it.

Every good gift and every perfect gift is from above, and comes down from the Father of lights . . .

—*James 1:17*

Action Jackson

Pet stores are intoxicatingly convincing that you *must* leave with a cute puppy. They can create the impulse buy of "cute" and leave you paying for that "cute" in installments in many different ways. Unfortunately, the mass sale of animals can invite the lowest common denominator of breeder to produce more animals quickly, without thought to bloodlines or humane, ethical treatment.

Puppy mills are a dangerous blight on animal breeding. Mothers and sons may be bred together, kept in cages only to reproduce, and shipped *en masse* to pet stores in hot trucks with no regard to the animals after the sale. Many puppy-mill animals find their way into stores, get top dollar, and end up in shelters, because when breeding is done irresponsibly, you can get animals with "a screw loose." Sometimes you get aggression, sometimes overly hyper behavior, and sometimes a physical malformation.

Jackson was an adorable buff cocker spaniel that was bought by a wonderful young couple. They did fine with him until their baby came along, and the dog refused to be housetrained. Jealousy over the baby and the attention that surrounded her caused the dog to become unruly and difficult. They didn't want to take the dog to a shelter, but they were running out of alternatives. You can't have a baby with a dog that continues to "leave presents everywhere."

That's when I got the call about Jackson. He was cute, sweet, and I knew immediately he was a puppy-mill dog. His eyes were a little crossed and his jaw was a little malformed. He was definitely going to be a handful for whoever ended up with him.

Attention was his middle name. Hyper was his last name. Jackson was all over the place. He was constantly being reprimanded, accompanied by the phrase "the fact that you are adorable is the only thing keeping you from being throttled." I honestly think that God has given unruly dogs "cuteness" as a defense mechanism to protect them from patience-strapped owners.

I placed Jackson in two different homes, and he came back to me both times. I call dogs like Jackson "boomerang" dogs, because they keep coming back. I thought he'd probably end up with me by default. He was too precious to take to the pound, and I was not about to give up hope on teaching him manners.

We went to obedience school. We crate trained. We watched videos on "I Am a Good Dog." We were getting nowhere. It's a very frustrating thing to love an animal but want to murder it at the same time.

I prayed for the right answer. Jackson was just not happy being part of a pack. He needed an overabundance of attention. He needed to be the only dog in a household. Bad behavior almost always stems from unhappiness. The most important role as animal caregiver is knowing when you have a happy animal and achieving happiness when you don't.

I was in a prayerful search for a happy environment for Jackson when I got a call from Kelly at Pampered Pets, the kennel where I leave my dogs when I'm out of town. A weekend assistant had spotted Jackson, and felt he'd be the perfect dog for her family in Kentucky.

As Jackson was driven away, my heart had a good feeling. It was the unspoken communication that the circuit had been completed. Somewhere inside, you know that this time, the adoption would be "just right." It was.

I got calls from the family saying that Jackson had integrated into the family as if he'd been theirs from birth. He ate at the table with them. He retrieved balls, gave loving kisses, and—*thank you, Lord*—practiced perfect housetraining. His obedience training kicked in, and they couldn't believe I had given them such a perfect pet.

Perfect is a word that describes that for which we feel unconditional love. No one, nothing is perfect as it stands naked to the world. Perfection comes to us in the gaze of someone who loves us. When we are accepted and loved for who we are, for everything we do, and in whatever mood we find ourselves, that is the moment of perfection. Jackson, in all his imperfections, found the perfect place to call home because his new family accepted him just as he was.

God loves us in our imperfection. But nothing we can do will erase that unconditional love and acceptance God has for us. So even if our eyes don't look quite right or we have a few screws loose—there is a family that always has open arms and the "adoption" is always "just right."

I'm grateful for that little cocker spaniel for leading me to realize that even in my unacceptable, raw state, there is Someone whose grace has made me perfect in His eyes.

Dogs love their friends and bite their enemies, quite unlike people, who are incapable of pure love and always have to mix love and hate.

—SIGMUND FREUD

Corky, the Yorkie

She was a three-pound tyrant of silk and barking sirens. Corky was a Yorkshire terrier that came to me through a friend who realized he'd made a mistake in buying her and trying to integrate her into his busy lifestyle. That happens a lot. People buy a pet on impulse and then realize the cute little puppy requires a lot of attention, not to mention housetraining. That's why countless purebred animals end up in shelters and pounds across the country.

A Yorkshire terrier had always been a want of mine, so when I saw the ad on the bulletin board at work, I immediately made my home hers. I had done research on Yorkies. I read everything that told me she'd be the perfect house pet. I had no idea what I was getting into. Corky was the only female in the house, other than me. She made herself queen of the castle by personally challenging my old Winston, the schnauzer, and Yogi, my golden. They were both so old that they let her think she was getting her way.

I never realized that the word *princess* probably came into being after spending an afternoon with a Yorkie. They are prissy and obnoxiously insistent with their barking, and simply must have all the attention in the house. She was just as adorable as she was a pain, which is why people put up with Yorkshire terriers in the first place. Take the word *terror*, make a few adjustments, and you get *terrier*. That will help you understand the temperament of these tiny, yet ferociously persistent creatures.

I did learn that every time Corky was put down on the floor, she began to bark. I would pick her up and the barking would stop. Down . . . she'd bark again . . . up . . . no bark. This little scenario played out daily, until I began carrying her around in the top of my overalls the entire time I was home. She liked that just fine.

In animal rescue, adoption, and fostering, it is probably more important to figure out the right placement for the right animal than anything else in the process. I realized quickly that I had made the same incorrect judgement about Corky as her original owner. She was a wonderful dog, just not a wonderful choice for me.

I began calling around to adoption agencies. I left word at my vet's and boarding kennel. The word was out, and I was honest: Corky was a handful!

When you are looking for homes for a pet, especially one you've grown attached to enough to carry them around in your pocket, you have to be careful. You have to let people know potential problems, so they won't end up with a dog that doesn't fit into their lives. I ran ads and screened them closely.

No . . . she couldn't live outdoors.

No . . . she couldn't live with a pit bull.

No . . . she wasn't a breeding possibility. (I had her spayed immediately.)

The questions one gets during adoption of a pet are just inane sometimes. But I got one call that seemed promising. A part-timer at the boarding kennel said she thought, perhaps, she had found a "mommy" for Corky.

Turns out, the potential mommy was the boarding tech's grandmother. Grandma was older and living with the tech's parents, who had been quite worried that she was getting a bit depressed. She wasn't going outside at all. She never wanted to walk around. She was just sitting in the house all day watching TV. They thought a little dog might cheer her up. I explained the hyper little Yorkie's habits, but that seemed to be more of a selling point than a hindrance. So Corky made her way to Kentucky.

Time passed and I heard nothing. I was beginning to worry and started the process of checking in to see how Corky the Yorkie was doing. I got a phone number, but never even had to make a call. I received a letter that day, in beautifully penned cursive writing, the kind southern ladies always used to have.

It was a thank-you letter from Corky's new mommy: "Thank you so much for my beautiful little angel. She has given me a reason to get up and walk every morning. We spend our days together. She has given me a reason to smile. She is such good company. Thank you so much for this wonderful gift."

Inside the letter was a picture of a stunning silver-haired lady, dressed for the holidays, holding another silver-haired lady named Corky in her sweet aging hands. They both seemed to wear the same brilliant smile.

There was no doubt that Corky was in the hands she was born for. And, if there are guardian angels who connect animals with their human soulmates, Corky had certainly been delivered to hers.

I got a couple of phone calls after that about Corky and how well she'd worked out in her new home, then none at all. There comes a moment of peace in the rescue and placement of animals when you realize that even if you weren't the final stop on the road to "home sweet home," you were definitely part of the plan to get them there.

*The Horse . . . here is nobility
without conceit, friendship
without envy, beauty without
vanity . . . a willing servant,
yet no slave.*

—RONALD DUNCAN

Juries

I drove to Loretto, Tennessee, to buy Juries, a sixteen-hand, sorrel brood mare, who in the sun looked like flames. She was an old foundation Tennessee Walking Horse, pregnant with a palomino baby, I hoped.

She'd been a family pet for many years and had given a whole herd of palomino horses to Mr. Bob Buerlein's brood.

I loved her from the minute I set eyes on her. I bought a trailer to take her home in. I drove as if she were nitroglycerine. It took me a whole day to get her home, but she didn't seem any the worse for wear after the trip.

Six months later she gave birth to a huge colt. He was named Big Gold Jury, but all my palomino hopes were dashed when he came out as bright sorrel as his mother. He had a white blaze and a stallion's personality from birth. His mother was amazing with him. There has never been, nor will there ever be, a more touching moment than that of a brood mare talking to her baby for the first time. The nuzzle, the warm kisses, and the trust are only found in those first moments of life.

Keeping horses is an expensive hobby, at best. And when you find that you can't keep your horses in good health and happy on your budget, you sometimes have to resort to some compassionate measures. Sadly, I realized that I would have to sell Juries and her colt. After Big Gold was weaned, I sold him through Jeff Givens, a trainer in Murfreesboro. Juries was a different story. She was old. I wanted her to be well cared for, and old horses don't always get that when they are sold.

I ran an ad with all the emotion I could muster. My first call was from a gentleman named Carroll. He was so kind. I sold Juries on the spot, and Carroll came for her the next week. He wrote me letters about how she was being spoiled and followed him everywhere.

As I got back on my feet financially, I never let go of missing Juries. She has tugged on my heart since the day I watched her with tears streaming down my face as the trailer pulled away.

I prayed, "Dear God, if you can just help me find her again . . . let me know she's all right."

The next day, God answered my prayer. I got a call from a listener to the radio show who said, "I saw your name on the papers for Juries. I own her now."

I burst into tears. "Is she all right? Is she doing okay?" I was so happy to get that call!

"She's pregnant with one of those palomino studs from down in Alabama. Think she'll be a great mama," he answered.

"What happened to Carroll?" I asked, referring to the man who'd bought Juries from me.

"He had some health problems, moved back to Texas," said the man on the phone.

"Did he take good care of her?" I wondered.

"Lord, yes . . . he'd have brushed her teeth and let her sleep in his house if he could have. Had tears in his eyes when we left with her," the new owner exclaimed.

"If you ever, ever, ever want to sell her, please call me first," I said.

"Well, of course, we will!" said the man, and he gave me his name and number.

If I never get to buy Juries back, God has given me enough to soothe the ache of not knowing where or how she is.

I always find that when we pray for something, God has an answer. Sometimes it's yes. Sometimes it's no. And sometimes, it's just the peace you get in knowing He's listening that makes all the difference.

All Living Creatures

Then God said, "Let the earth bring forth the living creature according to its kind: cattle and creeping thing and beast of the earth, each according to its kind"; and it was so. And God made the beast of the earth according to its kind, cattle according to its kind, and everything that creeps on the earth according to its kind. And God saw that it was good . . .

Then God blessed them, and God said to them, "Be fruitful and multiply; fill the earth and subdue it; have dominion over the fish of the sea, over the birds of the air, and over every living thing that moves on the earth."

—GENESIS 1:24-25, 28

*The best thing about a man . . .
is his dog.*

—*FRENCH PROVERB*

DJ, the Bug Dog

I met DJ when I was a volunteer at the Metro Pound in Nashville. Under its new director, it has become a much better animal control facility. But years ago it was considered one of the worst in the nation.

One day, as I walked through the dog runs, I saw a matted black and tan terrier-type dog. His hair was completely matted across his eyes, essentially blinding him. He sat there, wet and shivering. He was such a sad, stinky mess; no way was I going to leave him. When I walked out to pay his adoption fee, one of the attendants asked in disbelief, "You're going to take him?"

Of course I took him, and after bathing and clipping his fur, I found that this little dog was an Airedale. He was just adorable. Gaining his sight and having a nice warm bath or two changed his personality, much as it would mine, I'm sure.

His kennel cough, a common problem among adoptees from

damp multi-dog environments, was pretty severe, and he had developed an infection. So we visited the vet, and within a few weeks he was as good as new. He was completely housetrained, loved sleeping by the left side of the bed so I could reach his head with an occasional pat, and was in love with chasing and retrieving his little soccer ball. His name, for no particular reason, became DJ.

When I brought DJ home, I knew he would just be a temporary resident because, once again, I had far too many pets to take another. I ran ads. I announced him on the radio. I got no calls—not a one. I loved him to pieces, but somewhere I felt there was the perfect home waiting. I'm a firm believer that animals find us, not the other way around, so I left it to DJ to will the perfect human to us.

A few weeks later, the exterminator came to the house. DJ was fascinated with the "bug man." He followed him from room to room. He took him his toys. DJ was working his stuff for this guy, and I think he just charmed his way into the bug man's heart.

"What kind of little dog is this?" the bug man asked.

I explained he was a pound pup, with no bad habits, and that he needed a home. "He doesn't even shed, for goodness sake," I added.

"You know, I've always wanted a little dog to go with me on my bug route. You know, something to keep me company." I could see that the wheels in his head were turning. "I wonder if he'd like that?" the exterminator asked.

Then we started looking around the house for DJ. We called and searched to no avail. Then we walked outside and saw DJ, who had quietly slipped through a slightly open door and sat in the passenger side of the Bugmobile. I can't tell you what a sight he was, sitting there under the big roach on the roof of the car.

"Well, I guess that answers your question," I told the bug man, as he got in the van chuckling to himself.

Away they drove, DJ and the bug man, as happy as they could be. From what I hear, DJ still goes on the bug route every day and is great for repeat business.

From that shivering blind forgotten dog in the back of a kennel, to man's best friend, somehow DJ had found his calling in life, and I was just a stop along the way.

How can I help you . . . Say goodbye?

—KAREN TAYLOR-GOOD/
BURTON COLLINS

Steve's Baby Girl

People love their pets almost as much as they love their children. In fact, statistics tell us that more people actually have pets than have children these days. So I understood the hard place my friend Steve was in when he was forced to find a home for his beloved dog of many years.

He and his family were building a new house and had to live temporarily in an apartment that wouldn't accept pets. His old dog had been the love of his and his wife's life before they had children. The thought of saying goodbye to her was almost unbearable. He asked if I'd keep her. How could I say no?

This old girl was barely mobile. She had to be carried down the back steps so she could "do her business." Sometimes in her sleep, she'd urinate on herself. She couldn't hear or see very well. Though not in pain, she wasn't enjoying herself very much.

The most difficult stage of pet ownership is the responsibility to our faithful friends in the end stages of their lives. However, when is the right moment to say goodbye? We all pray that our old pets go peacefully in their sleep, naturally. Unfortunately, that doesn't always happen.

How do you tell a friend who loves his dog that she's ready to walk across the rainbow bridge? You don't. That decision can only be made by the heart that will be broken by the loss.

A few months later, Steve moved into his new house, and he brought his daughters to get his "girl." He was touched and moved by how old she looked and how feebly she moved. Time away has a tendency to remove blinders from all of us.

They went home amidst *thank-yous* and *we're-so-gratefuls*. I was happy to be able to help, but my heart hurt at the decision I knew Steve would be facing.

A few months later, I ran into Steve. I didn't even have to ask. His eyes misted over, and he said, "We had to put her down. I had no idea she had gotten so bad. I guess when you see a dog every day for so many years, you never see anything but the healthy, wonderful puppy she was when she came to you. The time at your house gave me a chance to really *see* her. I couldn't put her through any more life like that. We went as a family and kissed her goodbye. She got to at least spend a week with us in the new house."

I told him how sorry I was and what a wonderful old girl she was. He smiled.

"I would have never been able to do what I had to, if you hadn't given me a little time away from her. Thank you, for that," Steve said as he turned to leave.

The decision of compassion for our best friends is the hardest to make and the deepest sacrifice of love one can choose. For all who have had to make this choice, I am so sorry. But know that there is a place where all our good friends meet when they cross to the other side. They will be wagging their tails, chasing yarn balls, and banging their water buckets against their stalls when we see them again one day. I'm sure they will say thank you for being so kind to them.

I can only imagine heaven that way—it's one of the reasons I want to go.

Ever consider what they must think of us? I mean, here we come back from the grocery store with the most amazing haul . . . chicken, pork, half a cow. They must think we're the greatest hunters on earth!

—ANNE TYLER

Sophie's Choice Cut

There is a difference between wanting a particular breed of dog and the reality of owning one. I, being a woman of larger stature, had often loved the look of the long, tall women walking their Great Danes when I lived in New York. It was sophisticated, elegant, and striking. That began my desire to have one for myself (the dog, not the long, tall woman).

I gave it years, waiting until I owned a house with a fenced yard. I did a bit of research, clinging to the great qualities of this breed— and ignoring the bad ones. That's what we do when we are convinced in our hearts that we want a certain breed. We think, "My, that black and white dog will match my sofa." We say to ourselves, "I know he's huge . . . but he'll look great riding along in my car." Then reality sets in when you actually get that dog of your dreams.

Over the years, I'd seen families who'd insisted on getting a Dalmatian after seeing the movie *101 Dalmatians,* only to find real pups are messier and a lot more trouble than the cartoon ones. Apartment dwellers had insisted on border collies, who must have space to run and can become destructive if confined to an apartment. First-time pet owners had insisted on puppies. As a pet "know-it-all," I *tsk-tsked* as they chose an animal I knew would end up in a shelter or at a pet adoption center before the year was out. Me, however, I considered mistake-proof in the pet department.

I had my precious Winston, the miniature schnauzer, and my cat, Salem. I never consulted them on the idea of a new "ani-mate." They would love anything I brought home, right? Well, I figured I was mistake-proof in that department, too.

I searched through the ads for a Great Dane puppy. I found one at a huge discount because she was the runt of the litter. I drove to the town where the breeder was, and fell in love. Although I had been looking for the black and white color called harlequin, I settled for what is called Boston color, black with a white chest. She wasn't elegant at all. At eight weeks she was all feet and head. Her body already stretched across the entire front seat as I drove her home. And one of the "bad" characteristics that I had ignored—drooling— suddenly pinged in my memory bank. I thought, *I'd better go back and read that Great Dane book again, for real this time.*

Sophie got her name because she was the size of my sofa. You know, the one she matched perfectly? And the sofa was her favorite place to lounge. Lounging is an art perfected by the Great Dane. They do not sit. They do not lie down. They *lounge*. They stretch with their enormity across a comfortable plane, yawning loudly and snoring like a chainsaw. I have never seen anyone enjoy the comfort of lounging quite as much as this dog.

Her ears were clipped, and she wore the bandaged head casing for a little while, giving her the look of an alien space dog. She didn't seem to mind. In fact, one night, as I got out of my Jacuzzi after a relaxing soak, I turned to towel off and heard a huge *ker-splash*. I ran back to the tub to find Sophie in the middle of the bubble bath, bandaged ears and all, moaning with pleasure at the warm water and massaging jets. From that day forward, I had to make sure that the door to the bathroom was closed and locked when I was bathing. She had taught herself to turn the doorknob, and was fully capable of jumping right in the tub with me. As I said, these dogs are pleasure-gluttons. Sophie loved that hot tub, and for some reason developed a love for anything satin or cashmere. She could open drawers and pull out a garment, and I'd find her resting her head on the balled-up mass of what used to be a pair of silk pajamas.

Her baths were easy. She practically could be wiped clean with a washcloth. But anyone thinking a smooth-coated dog does not shed is quite mistaken. Another *ping* went off in my memory bank of disadvantages about her breed I'd ignored.

As for Winston and Salem, they were totally miffed about the new "alien." Salem, in fact, moved in with a neighbor. She was not about to be party to this disruptive nuisance. Winston, however, was not so lucky. Because Sophie was completely spoiled, letting her size determine where she went and what she got, she intimidated Winston into screaming submission on many occasions.

Sophie's chew bone was four feet long. You know the rawhide bones that people sometimes give as gag gifts to their boss at Christmas? Well, it was no gag gift for Sophie. She gnawed away at that baby until it was nothing but a gooey nub. One day she ran at me, with the chew bone covered in blood. I screamed and rushed her to the vet. He laughed as he announced, "Sophie's just lost her first baby tooth!"

"With all that blood?" I asked.

"Yes. Her baby teeth are just much bigger than most. There's gonna be some blood," my doctor assured me.

Her first heat was a major adjustment, too. I had never had a female dog before. And everything a normal-sized dog goes through happens to these gargantuan canines at about five times what you're used to. I rigged up some Depend undergarments for her. She was spayed immediately following this little medical fashion experience.

A Great Dane can always reach food you thought was completely beyond dog accessibility. She once walked by the kitchen counter and snarfed up four just-baked quiches I had cooling for a brunch party. I certainly had to punt for refreshments at that party. Thank you, Sophie! She once opened the refrigerator door and ate an entire roast. At least she closed the door when she was finished. She loved steak or any fresh raw beef, if it was a choice cut. Don't ask me how I found this out, or how long it took for me to learn the lesson of securing the refrigerator door with duct tape. Yes, my home had a lot of new "decorative" touches because of my mammoth baby.

When Sophie couldn't sleep, no one could sleep. She'd pounce on the bed. She'd whine. She'd put her glumpy old chew bone next to me in bed and gnaw away. Mind you, Sophie was well over a hundred pounds and, stretched out, was like another person on the bed. Some animal caregivers will probably get angry with me for what I'm about to relate, but they didn't have to live with Sophie when she was hyped up. From desperation, so I could get some sleep, I made her a screwdriver. I poured a small amount of orange juice and vodka with a little ice in her bowl. She loved it! Plus, she slept like a baby. The vodka did nothing for the fact that she snored like the neighbor's Weedeater, but she was at least sleeping. In some ways, it reminded me of taking a nap by my grandpa when I was a kid, so it was almost comforting.

Sophie was not a rescue. As I said in my introduction, this is not about the animals I have rescued, but those that have rescued me. Her story is not complete without praising her protective qualities, one of the good points the Great Dane book mentioned. I returned to my home one afternoon to find my screen ripped off the front window and blood on the windowsill. I rushed in to find the back door open and Sophie lying across the threshold with blood across the back door. I checked her for scrapes. I checked her for lost teeth. Apparently, as I found out when I called the police, there had been a rash of break-ins in the neighborhood. When my house was hit, Sophie was waiting. She was not hurt at all, but someone certainly got a "bit" more than they bargained for at my house.

One day I was doing my taxes in the middle of the living room floor, and I got a knock on the door.

"Who is it?" I asked.

"I'm from across the street," came the reply.

Assuming it was my neighbor, I opened the door a little, since I didn't have a peephole at that time. The door was pushed open and a man I had never seen before forced his way into the house. He was a tall dark man with gold-rimmed glasses and a green Army coat, and suddenly I knew I was in trouble.

"How did you like Chinese food last night? Was the pool game fun at the Sutler?" he asked, letting me know that he had followed me the night before. I'm 5'10" and fairly athletic, so I don't get frightened easily—but I was scared now. Winston was at the groomer's, so there was no loud yapping at his feet. Sophie, the sound sleeper that she was, was lounging in the back bedroom.

"I h-h-have a dog," I stammered.

"I'm not afraid of dogs," said the man as he started to move toward me. Other than the house across the street, there were no other houses in this new development. I was totally alone in the back of this subdivision.

"Sophie!" I yelled, and this big, black, foaming-drool beast hurled into the living room and pinned this man against the doorjamb. I grabbed her spike collar, leaving her growling, teeth gleaming about two inches from his face, a big paw on each side of his head.

"I don't guess you're into socializing right now," he barely whispered, fear in his voice.

"No, I'm not. Now please leave." I said, giving him just enough room to back out the door. Sophie stayed at that front door for days. I hadn't had her trained in any kind of attack work, but her obedience trainer said that came naturally to dogs. When they love you, they'll die for you. (There's no reason to train dogs to kill, which is a disservice to the dog.) Now, I know he was right. Twice, Sophie had saved me from harm.

Unfortunately, she didn't feel the same protective instinct with Winston. I had his ears sewn up on several occasions from run-ins with Sophie. He was old, and wasn't doing very well with Sophie as a housemate. I realized the most humane thing to do was to place Sophie in a one-pet household. I prayed for a home where she could be loved, given lots of attention, and be the only dog. She needed someone to protect.

Sophie first went to a home of a Great Dane owner who had lost her two Danes to old age. This woman then moved from a house to an apartment, so I got Sophie back. We tried her on a farm, but she boomeranged back when the people moved and had no place to keep her. Then my prayers for the perfect home for Sophie were answered. I got word of a woman who was afraid to leave her house because of domestic violence. We did some specific training through one of the police canine division officers who moonlighted a little on the side. Sophie was taught basic obedience commands and specific protection commands, but no violent tactics.

As the weeks went by after placement, I heard from Sophie through many channels. This woman and her family bought a special van so Sophie could go everywhere they went. She helped a woman gripped by fear begin to live a new life. Sophie was finally doing the job that she was sent to this earth to do. She was the star she was born to be.

Every person and every animal has a job on this planet. There is nothing nor anyone devoid of purpose. I learned so much from that big drooling angel. She taught me that not every breed is suited to everyone. I realized that just because a breed doesn't work out with you, it doesn't mean it won't be the answer to someone else's prayer. I understand now that matching a dog to a couch or an image isn't the most practical thing to do.

The last I heard, Sophie was on the way with her new family to Dallas to live in a house with a great big yard. I close my eyes sometimes and picture a lounging black dog, lying on a sofa somewhere, snoring . . . drooling . . . and loving every second of her life and adoring the people she's touched on her incredible journey.

Personally, I don't believe felines are a fad. We're here to stay.

—MORRIS THE CAT

Feedstore Fred

I was making an afternoon run to Garr's Feed in Mt. Juliet, on the outskirts of Nashville. I love the smell of a feed store. Seeds, leather from horse tack, and fertilizer all create the organic smell of days gone by. I always feel the urge to stick my hands in the seed bins and play with the dried butter beans as I did when I was a kid every time I hit the feed and seed place.

In the back, near the tweets of the baby chicks, behind the horse medicine, curled up on a burlap feed bag, was a striped yellow tabby. He began to follow me around the store, rubbing against me, purring, and begging to be picked up.

I did all my shopping that afternoon with "Fred" in my arms.

"You can have him, if you want. He just showed up here one day and he keeps ripping open the food bags," said the girl behind the counter.

I adored him already, so what was one more cat at the house? I bought a cat carrier along with the feed and horse supplies I needed, and away we went. The last time I tried to take a cat in a car without a carrier, it was like a scene from *Pet Sematary*, so I played it safe.

Since McCormick Animal Clinic was just at the end of my street, I dropped Fred off to spend the night, get his shots, and get neutered. I didn't want to expose my babies at home to a strange cat, in case he had any of those kitty immune diseases.

Fred came home with me the next evening. At home I set out his food bowl in the guest room away from the dogs or other cats. We cuddled a little bit and said good night.

The next morning, I walked in the guest room—no Fred. I called for him. I looked in the closet, under the bed, around all the furniture. Still, there was no sign of Fred.

As I began to look, I felt the breeze from the window opened just a few inches. Right in the middle of the screen, a hole had been torn just about the size of a cat.

Putting two and two together, I started piecing together the story that Feedstore Fred was probably telling all his friends somewhere in the neighborhood.

"You'll never believe what happened to me. I was just sleeping in the feed store, a veritable paradise for a cat, when this lady picked me up. She seemed nice enough until she put me in a cage and drove me to this place where I was poked and prodded. Then when I woke up, I was missing . . . missing . . . oh . . . I can't even say it." I imagine the cats leaning in, eyes big with fright.

"She put me in a room with some food and water, but as soon as I could find a way out . . . I grabbed it! Freedom! She seemed nice, but if in one night I'm missing these, what's going to happen tonight! I'm outta here!"

Sometimes an animal that is rescued says thank you, and sometimes it just says goodbye.

*Logic is death to that part of
you that is the miracle worker.*

—*STUART WILDE*

The Boxer of Mercy

I live in a quiet little neighborhood that respects leash laws and pet boundaries, so strays aren't a common occurrence. However, one day an unusual dog wandered down our street, a brindle boxer.

His skittish nature kept him at a distance, yet close enough for me to recognize he probably needed a meal and suffered from some sort of skin disease. I took food and water out to the middle of my yard, and after I walked into the house, he slowly walked over and ate and drank his fill. He looked at me as I stood at the window, then hurried off between the houses. I thought this was the last of my boxer encounter, as I assumed he probably belonged to someone.

Then a few days later, I heard a scratching at the front door. I opened it, and a matted dirty little cocker spaniel walked in. Out at the street stood the brindle boxer. He barked, and the little cocker barked back. Again, the boxer disappeared into the neighborhood.

I named the little cocker Dodi. I shaved her down, freeing her of the mats in her coat. I took her to the vet, who prescribed medication for a respiratory infection. After a few weeks, she was well, and a sweet wonderful part of our household. But unfortunately, I already had a household too full for Dodi. After running ads in the lost and found, I used word of mouth and placed Dodi with a wonderful couple who still keeps in touch about their precious "girl."

Some weeks later, I heard another scratching at the door. A matted black cocker spaniel, obviously quite sick, was waiting when I opened the door. At the street again was the brindle boxer. He barked, the black cocker walked in my house, and the boxer disappeared just like before, as if he had brought the dog to me for help. The same process was repeated as with Dodi: vet, shaving, cleaning, healing, and naming. Manfred was quite a handful, but a sweet beautiful dog by the end of the month. Through friends we found a new owner who drove down from Indiana to get him. He's now an only child in a wonderful home.

About a month later, scratching at the door was a reddish blond Heinz-57 full of energy and pep. Again, there was that brindle boxer who had delivered her to my door. Darlene, as I named her, was suffering from cancer. I'm sure she had been dumped for that reason. Luckily, it was a treatable form, and she now happily resides with me (more about her later). She's a happy dog that loves the farm and horses and sleeping under the bed.

A few others have been brought to my house by the brindle boxer. All were sick and hungry. All are now in wonderful loving homes. It's funny—I've never so much as patted the old boxer on the head. I guess somewhere in the deep soul of a dog, it can sense someone willing to help. I haven't seen him in a year or so, but somewhere I know he's waiting. He's waiting until another dog comes along that can't survive without help. He's waiting to do his job on this earth.

One day, he'll appear, and a scratch on the door will yield a new baby who needs loving. Is he a dog? An angel in fur? Or are his apparent "deliveries" just coincidences?

I don't know the answer, but I do know that when I hear that familiar bark, it will be impossible not to open the door and answer his call.

*People that hate cats will come
back as mice in their next life.*

—*FAITH RESNICK*

Tramp-man, Travis' Cat

My friend Judy from JuRo Stables called me and said, "I've got some kittens that need homes, but one's been hurt really badly by a horse. Can you help me?"

It didn't take long before I was bound for Mt. Juliet. For some reason when someone says he or she needs help with a dying animal, I am tireless. It's the adrenaline rush of all time to try to save a hurt cat or dog. When I arrived at the stables, I lost hope immediately, however, because the kitten had been crushed.

His tail was hanging on by a thread; he couldn't walk because his pelvis had been destroyed. He was just screaming and crying. Nothing other than a child in pain can evoke such hurt in my own heart. I made a beeline to my vet's while calling ahead on my cell phone.

This kitten's pelvis was crushed, but internally he wasn't hurt too badly. I had Dr. McCormick perform surgery and remove the tail, which had already begun to rot from infection. All we could do was hope, pray, and give this kitten a lot of love and attention.

Antibiotics, special feedings, and lots of aloe and hydrogen peroxide began the healing process. But that began another problem none of us had thought about. A cat with a broken pelvis couldn't use a litter box. He was still in pain in the pelvic area while he was healing so he couldn't strain either. Not to be graphic, but any creature who takes in, must let out, or it will die. So this was a serious problem.

I thought back to the slumber parties that friends had thrown where someone had been "coaxed" into wetting the bed by putting her hand in warm water while she slept. I wondered if that could be modified to get the "works" going for Tramp. He was covered in fleas, so maybe I could kill two birds with one stone.

I held him by the scruff of his neck and lowered the bottom part of his body into warm water in the sink. He struggled and screamed for about a second, then he relaxed because it felt so good. It wasn't much longer before the body functions were completed. Everything worked like a charm. He was so tiny that it wasn't as bad a procedure as it sounds. In a few weeks, he was healed enough to climb into the small litter box I'd made.

In the meantime, Diane, the assistant at Dr. McCormick's office, called. Her son had fallen in love with Tramp during his stay at the vet. He had to have that cat. So the adoption was made—and Tramp-man became a little boy's best bud. Because a cat without a tail doesn't have much balance, many funny stories and adventures resulted about Tramp *not* being able to always land on his feet. Tramp certainly repaid his debt in love to this little boy.

In life, there will be many hopeless cases. There are times when the future is so bleak there is not even a glimpse of the sun. Sometimes, we are given bad prognoses by doctors, we are in financial rubble, and we are lonely. However, when love and patience join as one, there are no hopeless cases. For every negative rule there is a positive exception.

It is an amazing thing that a kitten, crushed and hurt, taught me one of the greatest lessons of all—hope.

Don't accept your dog's admiration as conclusive evidence that you are wonderful.

—ANN LANDERS

Darlene, the Trailer Park Queen

The familiar scratching on my front door had become commonplace in my life. The pet hotline in the universe somehow delivers animals in need to the people who help them—and vice versa.

Darlene and I were given to each other. She was red with blond underneath and looked remarkably like a fox. The oddest thing about this little red dog was her smile. This dog actually looked up at me and smiled as she pranced right into my house. It was at a time when I most needed a smile too. If I could have prayed "light" back into my life, Darlene most definitely could have been an answer to that prayer. We found that she had cancer, but chemo healed her fully—just as she began to heal the "cancer" that had been eating away at my spirit for years. I don't know who felt more healed after a few months together.

Mixed in heritage and breeding, yet bearing more intelligence than most people I know, Darlene won my heart and that of everyone she came in contact with. The folks at Pampered Pets, the kennel where she stayed while I was away, *loved* her. At the vet clinic, she was the favorite. Anyone in her company smiled and instantly felt better. If any animal or being on this earth deserved the title "angel," it would have to be Darlene. Of course, that quality kept me from losing it when her maddening habits began to show.

Darlene was an escape artist. A six-foot privacy fence was no deterrent to her. She could dig out, move cement blocks, and manage to wriggle out of any space. She was "born to be wild," or at least born to visit all the neighborhood dogs who weren't smart or wily enough to escape their outdoor prisons. In the time it took for me to let her out the back door to "do her business," she could manage to dig a bit each day on her route to freedom. Each five-minute constitutional got her closer. Then there would be the fateful five minutes of her last dirt dig out of the back yard, and she'd be gone. I could take my eyes off her for a second, and she'd disappear—into thin air it seemed.

I'd run to my Jeep and take off into the neighborhood, and she'd be waiting on a corner. I always thought this little game of hers was simply a way to get a private "mommy and me" ride, which she dearly adored. Because Darlene had such a penchant for running away, she wore a collar with her name and my phone number engraved on a little red heart. Sometimes when she wasn't waiting on a corner, I'd get a call from the Cracker Barrel down the street. Darlene would be sitting outside greeting the customers.

I'd pick her up and everyone sitting in rockers out front would chorus, "Goodbye, Darlene!" Darlene made friends wherever she went. It was her special gift on earth. I truly believe that Darlene belonged to everyone. One time I got a call from the car wash down the street, and Darlene was playing in the water and trying to get someone, anyone, to take her for a ride.

The vet clinic would call, because Darlene had stopped by for a "visit." People in the neighborhood would call and tell me that Darlene had come by and spent the night. You might think me an awful pet owner, to have lost her so many times. However, that is how Darlene came to be mine in the first place. She just knocked on my door and walked in.

It seemed everyone knew her and loved her. She didn't ever meet a stranger, and she never met anyone she didn't instantly love.

She was like the good old gal that you knew from the trailer park who had a heart of gold and a family tree with fruit of every kind hanging on it. If she were a person, she'd have smoked Kools, laughed uproariously at everything, been divorced six times from men who still loved her dearly, and have had a rose tattooed on her behind. She would have known all the good gossip, but never have told a word.

My dear friend Sharon had been caring for her ailing mother for quite a few years until she passed away. In a deep depression, Sharon called and told me that without her mother's presence in the house she was simply unable to function.

"I need something to take care of. I think I need a dog," she said, crying uncontrollably.

"Before you go adopt a dog, let me give you Darlene. She's got a special way of making people smile again. It's her gift from God. If any dog could heal you, it'd be my baby. If it works out, she was supposed to be yours. If it doesn't . . . you'll just end up happy again, and she'll come back home to me. Deal?" I asked.

As normal for all my adoptions, I bought a new leash, bowl, and dog food. I took Darlene over to Sharon's house, and Darlene began her magic.

"She smiles!" Sharon exclaimed.

"I know," I said as I left the two of them to become friends.

Two weeks passed, and I got a desperate call from Sharon.

"Come get this dog! She's just not working out. I love her, but there is hair everywhere!" Sharon was totally exasperated with her canine Candystriper.

"I'll be right over," I said with a smile. I didn't tell her that I'd cried every night for two weeks missing my little "Weenie," as I affectionately called Darlene.

When I came in the house, Darlene ran and jumped from the floor to my arms. She was ready to go home. Her work there was finished.

"You cannot believe the places dog hair can get," Sharon complained. She began to recount the hair hell she'd been in, when a funny thing happened. Sharon's sense of humor, which is deadly funny when in full capacity, started revealing itself. She laughed a big belly laugh over her two weeks of Darlene escapades. She told how Darlene lounged alone at home on the off-limits couch watching *Animal Planet*. She told how this dog somehow always wound up snuggled up next to her in bed by morning. And as she told me of all these horrors, she continued to laugh.

"Have you realized what's happened, Sharon?" I asked.

"I . . . I'm laughing," she said in amazement.

For a month, my friend who'd been unable to get out of bed with depression and tears, was not only out of bed, but laughing, complaining, cleaning, and living again. Darlene again had spread sunshine to someone.

"I don't guess I really need to own a dog; I just needed to rent one!" Sharon waved us off from her front door.

Darlene went home with me that night, and we snuggled as I told her what a great job she'd done in healing Sharon. She smiled as if she understood what I was saying.

A few months later Darlene dug out from the fence in the backyard during her five minutes of play time. I ran to my Jeep to catch her at the corner, but she wasn't waiting there. I drove around the neighborhood off and on for the rest of the night. No Darlene.

The next day on our radio show we announced that she was missing, and several people called in. She was all over the neighborhood. I'd go to find her, and I'd get to her location just after she'd gone. All the neighbors helped. She was spotted everywhere. The only place she wasn't spotted was with me. It was as if she'd just disappeared.

Well, I knew if someone found her, her collar would tell the finder who to call. I went to the fence where she had dug out—and there was the little collar with the red heart with her name, in the dirt, where she'd pulled it off. I began to panic. This began a daily venture to the pound and the shelters, and searches through newspaper ads and the Internet.

I heard over and over how I should have put a microchip in her, so she could be located easily. Yes, I heard everything I should have done. Now, along with the huge pain of loss, I also felt great guilt. It was my fault. I should have watched her more closely. It didn't matter that she'd dug around the cement I'd poured to keep her in. It didn't matter that she was only out for a few minutes. It didn't matter that I'd looked everywhere. She was gone, and I blamed myself.

The kennel help cried when I told them. The vet clinic staff was saddened to lose its pal. The neighbors all told me stories of "my little smiling" dog. I soon realized that she really was everyone's dog, and everyone was going to miss her.

I have learned that there are many things one can do to keep from losing a pet. I have learned there are a host of things I should have done differently. But none of that has brought Darlene back, so I've had to come to a compromise within myself. For the three years she'd chosen me, I gave her the best home I could have possibly given her. I did my best. She just wasn't supposed to be mine forever.

Perhaps Darlene came to me to spread some joy in my world, when I didn't have any of my own. Or could it be that her entire job on this earth was to help my friend Sharon come to grips with saying goodbye to her mother and introducing her to life again. Maybe Darlene wasn't a dog at all, but just a beautiful, gypsy spirit who taught every human she touched how to smile, then disappeared into the mists that brought her.

I do not know how she came to me or where she has gone. But every night I say a little prayer, that somewhere, someone who was needing a smile heard a scratching at her door, and opened it to find a little red dog with a contagious zest for living. I picture Darlene, curled up by a fireplace at the feet of someone who no longer has an empty place in her heart because of an "angel with fur" who knocked on her door.

It is that picture of Darlene that lets me fall asleep—with the smile that she brought me, when she knocked on my door.

And she said, "Yes, Lord, yet even the little dogs eat the crumbs which fall from their masters' table."

—MATTHEW 15:27

A Dobie's House

I was judging some of the competitions at Dog Fair Day in Centennial Park in Nashville, which raised money for the Humane Association. The whole event was something I greatly looked forward to. After my duties were done, I walked around to look at the exhibits.

Big mistake, if you don't want to end up with another dog at your house. As I walked to the booth for Golden Retriever Rescue, I was struck by the saddest picture of a golden that needed fostering. She was suffering from heartworms and abuse, but would need six months of care before she could be placed. The fair was ending, and I seemed to be the last resort for the rescue team. After a game of twenty questions—grueling ones, I might add—they decided that I was a suitable candidate for fostering.

I have been through the heartworm treatment process with many animals, and they had all lived through it. As long as they are kept quiet during the long recuperation, most dogs come through fine. Heartworm treatment, you see, is often as bad as the disease. It's a poison shot directly into the bloodstream, which goes to the heart to kill the parasites. It greatly compromises the heart function, and if excited, the dogs can die of a heart attack early in the medicine's effectiveness. I knew what was in store, but I had faith we'd both be fine.

At the vet clinic I asked for Dobie. When they brought her out, her hair was missing in great clumps. She crawled out to the waiting room on her belly. She shied away from all human touch. These signs of abuse were much worse to me than the results of the heartworm treatment. It always breaks my heart to see abuse in any form, but I think there must be a special place in Hades for someone who can hurt a golden, the sweetest spirits of the animal kingdom.

Dobie adapted well to my other dogs. They were so used to fosters in and out, they didn't even bark at her. After a few welcome sniffs and a warning over their individual food bowls, we were a family.

It took weeks before Dobie would come to me without cowering. I just kept loving her, bathing her in soothing skin baths, and gently working with her in basic obedience commands. I never raised my voice and praised her constantly. I truly believe that all pain, human or animal, can be loved away. Dobie was living proof of that.

In the meantime, a friend told me about getting an e-mail from some friends in North Carolina. They just loved goldens and were thinking about adopting one. "Funny you should be looking now, because I have a friend with one who needs a home," she wrote back.

Adoption and placement often happen like that. A friend tells a friend, who tells a friend, who tells a friend, and across miles a need and a desire meet and go home together. That is exactly what happened to Dobie. The happiest and saddest moment are both the instant you see a creature you have loved for a time, looking back at you through a back windshield as he is driven to his new home. It never gets easier to say goodbye, and at no time does anything make me quite as joyful.

I watched Dobie, her tail wagging in the back seat of the little red car on the way back to North Carolina, her chew bone in her mouth. It had been an instant bond between the new adoptive mommy and Dobie. That's how you know it's the "right fit" in the adoption process. The animal instinctively goes where it loves and is loved. Usually the animal gives a quick look back to its foster parent to "say thank you," then is held fast in the arms of "home."

Dobie keeps in touch through her adoptive mom's e-mail. I know that she's helped her human through police academy training and the trials of a difficult marriage. Dobie's hair has grown back beautifully, covering any evidence of past abuse. As many adoptive animals do, she devotes her entire life to showing gratitude to the new person who daily puts space between her new home and a horrible past.

The most important thing I learned from Dobie, and all the other transient hearts that have let me in, is that love, not time, heals all wounds. God's animal creatures instantly know a good heart when they see one. They know when someone is trying to help them and they accept it. They never ask for more than you can give and always give more than you ask.

It is that precious knowledge that gives me the strength to say *yes* to all I can, and the strength to say *goodbye* when the time is right.

*Dogs need to sniff the ground; it's
how they keep abrest of current
events. The ground is a giant dog
newspaper, containing all kinds of
late-breaking dog news items, which,
if they are especially urgent, are
often continued in the next yard.*

—DAVE BARRY

The Football Fan

It was the first game of the Women's Pro Football league in Nashville. It was cold, and people lined the stands. Then an announcement was made, "Get the dog off the field."

A huge German shepherd was running around the field, pregame, trying to get someone to play with him. He was really becoming a nuisance, and I heard one of the officials say, "Call animal control."

Ever since I saw the Disney movie version of an animal control officer, I've been fear-struck at the thought of sending any animal to a "pound." On an impulse I hopped up and shouted, "I'll take him!"

So I pulled my Jeep around and loaded in seventy-five pounds of strange shepherd. After the game, I got in the car with this huge slobbering dog, and the reality of what I had done set in. I did not know this dog. I didn't know if he would bite. I didn't know if he was comfortable riding in cars. I knew nothing!

I got home, a little shaken over the ride with Cujo, and put him in my fenced-in backyard. I got him fresh water, fed him, and patted him on the head. There was a padded igloo outside to keep him warm, so I thought he'd be fine.

A trip to the grocery store later, I went out to check on my new ward. I called, "Here, puppy." No response.

I looked under the deck. No dog.

How could a seventy-five pound dog disappear from a backyard with a locked privacy fence? Then I looked at the gate. Right in the center, at the bottom, was a hole. It had been ripped and chewed to the size and shape of a seventy-five pound German shepherd. He'd literally chewed his way to freedom.

I was busy reprimanding myself for bringing the dog home in the first place, as I drove around the neighborhood looking for this behemoth. I looked all afternoon to no avail.

This was just great. I'd missed the ball game, gotten a few hundred dollars in damage done to my privacy fence, and lost the dog. Pretty much, I considered it a loser day.

Two weeks later, I was driving down the street when I saw a huge German shepherd "walking" an owner down the sidewalk. It was my behemoth! And he was tugging with all his weight by his leash, while his waif of a walker ran gasping behind.

I could have stopped. I could have said, "I'm sorry . . . he chewed out of my gate." I could have helped her walk this beast. However, I decided that God had delivered this dog to his rightful owner, and both seemed happy—and well exercised, at that!

I guess it goes to show you that animals choose their owners, no matter how high the fence or how short the leash. Why argue with fate? At least, I have peace in knowing that the dogcatcher had a little less to do that Saturday.

Use what talents you possess,
The woods would be very silent
If no birds sang, except those who
sang best.

—HENRY VAN DYKE

Big-haired Bernice

When pet stories are told, birds often get left out. They sing to us, and talk to us, and give us great entries in the "Funniest Home Videos" competitions. But while cats purr, and dogs nuzzle, and ponies nicker softly—birds screech loudly, and, depending on the size of the beak, have the ability to snap your fingers off.

I knew all this, yet I could not wait to have an African gray parrot. I wanted an intelligent animal that could talk to me. Now, I must tell you, when your life has gotten so empty that you are trying to find pets to have con ersations with you, it is time to get out of your house! As Jerry Seinfeld used to say about people getting monkeys, "*Go ahead and have a kid!*" A big bird is much like having a kid. They must have food, toys, and a clean place to sleep, and they can throw tantrums about any of the aforementioned at any time. How do I know? In one word—Bernice.

At the closing of the Tennessee Bird Fair, a quarterly bird "flea market" held at the State Fairgrounds in Nashville, people were packing up, ready to hit the road, and I was on a mission—a parrot mission! I was determined to leave with a bird that could talk to me. I had been told that at the end of any show people are trying to go home with less than they came with, so they'd be ready to deal. Well, a deal I found, indeed! There she was, in a cage, cooing gently to the man who was selling her. She was so sweet to him.

"She was hand-fed, my little girl, JoJo," the man said of his African gray baby. She had papers and everything. She'd be a wonderful breeder too. This animal was so affectionate with him.

"But does she talk?" I asked in hopes of my dream coming true.

"Talks a blue streak," he answered with a smile. "But you gotta teach her."

I was all over that, as I wrote him a check for the cage, the food, and the toys and walked awkwardly to my truck with all of it. I was elated. I was a big bird owner. I stopped and bought care books and more toys. It was as if I were coming home from the hospital with a precious bundle, but instead of a baby—I had the stork!

After getting her set up in my house, in her own room with greenery and a big picture window, I opened her cage. In my fantasy, she would walk out and perch on my finger and say, "I love you." My dream was punctured about the time her immense beak clamped down on my finger like a buzz saw and vise combination. I could *not* get her to let go. It hurt like she was trying to take my finger by force. I couldn't shake her loose. I squirted her with the water bottle I found with my left hand. I was permanently attached to this bird with searing pain, it seemed. When all hope of prying, shaking, or pleading her loose were dashed, I used what has gotten me out of most scrapes. I hollered.

Now if you are from the city, *scream* might be the word used. But if you are a country girl, like me, *scream* is far too delicate for what I did.

I got in this infernal animal's face and hollered. It was close to what my grandmother would have called a "beller." But it worked. I think Bernice, which I named her instead of JoJo, was about as shocked as I was with the whole experience. The holler-let-go technique was quick and it worked the first time. I was not going to ever test it a second time.

Soon I found that Bernice loved "input." She loved television, radio, the sound of the answering machine—anything that gave her communication. She'd cock her head, her eyes would dilate, and she'd learn phrases. Her favorite input was from the African-American church services and the gospel great CDs I had of Mahalia Jackson and the Fairfield Four.

"Praise Gawwwd!" she would say as she sang, puffed, and head-bobbed to the music and preachers. I have never known such a spiritual bird. She also seemed to enjoy when I wheeled her cage in so she could watch a Discovery Channel special on African grays.

I bought her a special $300 perch that was the Cadillac of perches. It was like a banyan tree in the living room. I presented it to her, opening her cage, this time with oven mitts on up to my shoulders. Bernice was horrified of this thing. She not only wouldn't go near the perch, but ran screeching from the room, and hid under the armoire in the hallway until I got the perch completely out of the house. It became a rack for drying delicates next to the laundry sink in the garage.

She hated new toys, she hated new food, and she hated me. In six years of coaxing, trying, teaching, and singing, I had to face the fact that I was not going to get affection from this animal.

Of course, this book is about animal rescue, but I bet you didn't think there would be a story about me being rescued *from* one of my animals! I took Bernice to be boarded at McCormick Animal Clinic, and I warned them of her quick tease, flirt, and attack methods. I told them all the things she hated, and all the reasons to be wary of this bird.

I arrived after a week to find Bernice riding around on Dr. McCormick's shoulder. She was puffed up and flirting with him, much as she had done with her previous owner.

Bernice was in love!

"You go, big-haired girl!" she would shout as she passed me atop her love-nest perch. This bird was in heaven.

The people in the waiting room reacted in laughter at the sight of the vet with a bird on his shoulder. Bernice began saying *hello,* and making the sound of the door's sentry bell every time someone would walk in.

"Do you want her?" I asked in a moment of happiness at the sight of the bird I wished I'd found at my house for the last six years.

"Oh, these birds are so expensive," the crew at the vet hospital exclaimed.

"She's free, if you want her," I said to their nods of approval.

Now Bernice is fed grapes and Cheetos and lives in a parrot condo with an activity "spa" atop, and a cockatiel that keeps her company in the vet office. She visits with patients and their owners and keeps conversation up as long as you aren't looking at her. She dances to *Chattahoochee,* and still loves the "boys" in the office. I visit from time to time, and stare in wonder at the only animal that I have ever had that wanted me dead.

Bernice taught me that love cannot ever be forced, bought, or achieved simply by wanting it. We cannot ever love enough to gain love where it is not. Love can't be earned and it can't be manufactured. And she taught me that sometimes the kindest thing to say to someone or something you love is goodbye.

The average dog is a nicer person than the average person.

—ANDY A. ROONEY

Over-the-road Max

He was silver and shaking and wanted to go home. There in the back of the shelter was Max, a miniature schnauzer listed as unadoptable. Max had tested positive for heartworms and was on the euthanize list.

I hate when people consider a dog with heartworms "over." Heartworms can be treated successfully. It is not an easy procedure: it isn't always successful, and, yes, it is expensive. But I have never considered a $250 risk as too much.

Max went home with me, and we went through the heartworm procedure like a charm. He left Dr. McCormick's healthy and ready for his new home. He went home with Gerry and Allyson House, and became a big part of their family in Mt. Juliet.

They went for walks, and Max became a good partner for Ed, their Yorkie. When they moved into town, Max didn't make the transition from country to city very well, so we found a new home.

Although animals are part of our lives, sometimes an animal is happier in a particular environment. People are like that. The wide-open-spaces people aren't happy in a high-rise, and the high-rise people hate the "sticks." Animals are just like us in that way.

Finding a home for a pet you love isn't the easiest thing. You almost always have "giver's remorse" as you watch your baby ride away with someone, but Max's story is wonderful.

Max was adopted by an over-the-road truck driver who takes him all over the country on his route. Never have you seen a happier dog than Max, with his head stuck out of that big rig.

For a while, Max's new dad would call the radio station and give us reports. But as in all things, the old ties fade and the new ones set in, and Max became part of a new family.

In animal rescue, there are often many ports before a safe harbor is reached. All are a necessary part of the journey and none is more important than the other. Often we opt not to be a port, because we feel we can't offer a permanent solution. But if all we do is offer a temporary home, pay a vet bill, or pick up a hurt animal on the road-side and take him to a shelter, we have done what we were commissioned by God to do.

Stories can't have a happy ending without a beginning or a middle, and sometimes we are only called to be a "middle." Max has shown me the importance of creating a chain of love. Every kind action leads to another and another. If we all begin each day with a kind action, chances are the chain will reconnect to us by the end of the day. Whatever order we are in the links of the chain, we are integral to the connection of that chain in the plan of the universe.

And in the case of Max and all the links of his chain of love, they all lived happily ever after.

She knows that nine lives are enough.

—OSWALD BARRON

KT's Pink Collar

My friend Whitney was having a "clearance" sale of clothes and furniture before moving from Nashville to Los Angeles to work for Madonna's new publishing company. Somewhere between trying to squeeze into her shoes and fighting over designer handbags, I saw two beautiful black cats curled up on a pile of cashmere sweaters in a chair.

"Who are these babies?" I asked. Since Belshazzar, I have had a fondness for black cats.

"Well, the big one I call BC, short for Big Cat," answered Whitney. "And the other one doesn't really have a name. She's his sister. I found them in a dumpster and they've been mine ever since. Perfect acquisition, since I have two white couches!"

"They are going to love L.A., as laid back as they are," I said, considering they hadn't moved or even acknowledged the presence of the ongoing hen party.

"Oh, I can't take them. Could you please help me find a home for them or at least take care of them until I can get set up and send for them?" The bell had rung and the shoe had dropped. Whitney knew an easy mark.

"Of course," I replied, without a second thought. When you have as many animals as I often had in the house, what's one more?

Cats who have never known dogs don't often socialize very well. You have to give them plenty of "getting to know you" time, and put litter boxes in odd hidden-away places. If you don't make sure that Kitty has a place away from possible menaces to "go," Kitty will go without the aid of a litter box. I'd rather endure a litter box on a recessed high bookshelf for a while than the alternative. It took about two weeks before the cats ignored the dogs, just as they had the hen party.

BC weighed about eighteen pounds. He looked as if a normal cat's head had been stuck on an inflatable one that had been blown up to triple its size. The only time I ever heard from BC was at feeding time. (That translated into any time I would walk into the kitchen.)

On the other hand, his no-name sister followed me sassily from room to room protesting everything. If you picked her up, she howled. If you let her down, she meowed like death. She adored being cuddled and was a ball of teddy bear when she wanted to be. KT was one of the few cats I've known that demanded to be held.

Curling up in the bathroom sink was one of her favorite things, especially on busy mornings when I was trying to get ready for work. Attention was her middle name. KT, in honor of song diva K.T. Oslin, became her first name. She was a sassy cat, and if K.T. the singer ever came back as a cat, this one would be it.

After a year, I realized Whitney was probably not going to send for her cats, which didn't bother me much, since I'd become quite attached. They seemed to love going outside and bird watching.

Cats often live somewhere for a while, then they decide they'd rather take up residence somewhere else. That was the case for BC. Soon, I noticed he was spending a lot of time down in the cul-de-sac with a neighbor, only coming home when he heard me open the feed bin. Those coming-home times became fewer and further between, until he took up permanent residence with his new family. His new family loved him, and loved him the way he wanted to be loved. The last time I saw him, he was at least a couple of pounds heavier.

KT, on the other hand, stayed with me, remaining as talkative as ever. She stayed curled up on her favorite spot, the woodpile on the front porch, where she'd stay until we had "cuddle" time each night.

In the summer I got new neighbors, Rick and Ron. They were a delightful pair with a wire-haired Jack Russell terrier named Mallory. KT often went on walks with them around the neighborhood. Pretty soon, KT's favorite place was no longer the woodpile at my house, but the front porch of Rick and Ron's. Then KT moved inside the house and became a part of the family. The guys were a bit apologetic about "taking" my cat, but they seemed to love her so much, and bought her a little pink collar.

She would stop by from time to time, but only for a moment. The guys said she would sit by the sink and watch them get ready, talking constantly. She'd follow them from room to room in a highly vocal state.

A few months later, Rick and Ron moved to another house down the road, and KT went with them—for a while. She didn't seem to make the change very well. She was constantly trying to get back in the house Rick and Ron had moved from. Then one day, I opened my front door, and there was KT, her little pink collar shining in the sun. She wasn't moving, and sat staring off into nothingness. I picked her up, and she stiffened. She was alive, but there was definitely something wrong.

I didn't even take the time to find the guys, I just rushed KT to the emergency vet clinic on 12th Avenue. They took one look at her and asked if she'd been having seizures.

The familiar feeling I had during my old schnauzer Winston's last days came back to me. His seizures were awful, and I will never forget the helpless inability to do anything for him. Here I was in the same boat with KT, and she'd come home to me because she knew there was something wrong.

"Her ears are yellow inside. A yellow cat never lives very long," said the young veterinarian on staff.

"Please, *do* something," I asked. He saw I was desperate to keep her out of pain.

"It's her liver, isn't it?" I remembered what liver failure looked like because I'd been through it with Winston.

"Let's not panic. I'll get her on some fluids on an IV and see what we can do to save her. I'm not making any promises though. She is . . . a yellow cat, you know?" he said, doing his best not to worry me, yet not filling me with false hope.

"Yes, I know . . . yellow cat." I left with that sick feeling of truth in my stomach. You know when as a pet guardian you are being tugged on to make the decision of the kind, gentle act of letting go.

Twenty-four hours later, I sat in the Hermitage Animal Hospital and made that decision. The veterinarians were all amazing. They gave me goodbye time.

It is in the moments of goodbye to a loved part of your life that you realize your own meaning. As we all wind down to our last breaths, it is not important where we live, what we have accumulated, or what we have achieved that matters. Even God's animal creatures realize that coming home and being in the arms of love are the only send-off we yearn for.

She was purring loudly as she went to sleep. I picture her curled up on the ottoman at some angel's feet. Do animals go to heaven? Of course! How could a place be called heaven, if there wasn't the unconditional love of our pets to greet us at the gate?

I am grateful for that dumpster kitten that made her way to me, and back to me later in life when she needed to feel the comfort of home around her. She taught me that home is a *who*, not a *where*. I realized after KT that we all need someone who represents home to us. On my piano where KT used to love to sit in the sun is a shiny black urn, and around the urn is a collar in her favorite shade of pink.

The reason a dog has so many friends is that he wags his tail instead of his tongue.

—ANONYMOUS

Manfred's Trip to Indiana

Manfred was a delivery from the Boxer of Mercy. He was a black cocker spaniel, cold, damp, and matted from exposure to the elements. I opened my door and he ran in shivering.

I didn't hesitate to throw him in the tub. He was so cold, the warm water ran over him and warmed him instantly. After his bath, I began shearing him down to get rid of the mats that covered his ears and eyes.

Manfred cleaned up quite nicely and was purple ebony color with a finely chiseled head and a wagging "tootsie roll" of a tail. He was lovable and full of cocker spaniel energy. He had no collar and had obviously been on the road a while. He ate voraciously. He sucked down water as if he'd been in a desert. He slept in front of the fireplace as if he'd finally found his home.

He got a purple collar the next day with his name and my phone number. I ran an ad looking for his owners to no avail, so I began running an ad to find him a good home. Manfred and Henry, my schnauzer, became fast friends. They romped and played like mates. Henry would growl and complain, and Manfred would goofily pounce around him as if it mattered not. He knew Henry was all growl and no bite.

As I opened the front door one day, the two of them scooted past me running for a break of freedom. I ran after them, but lost them behind some houses. I have never understood the joy with which dogs run away from their masters. They look back as if to laugh, knowing that getting away from you is just so easy!

I got a call within a half-hour from a lady a block away, who had my little black misfits in her back fenced-in area. I was there in two minutes, and she asked me about Manfred.

"I have a sister who is looking for a black cocker spaniel. She might get a puppy," said the kind lady who'd captured my "mongrels."

"You know he's up for adoption?" I asked her.

"Really?" she asked. "My sister lives in Indiana, though."

"I don't mind driving, if she'd give him a good home," I answered.

It was a twenty-four hour decision and an eight-hour drive each way, but Manfred now has a home in Indiana.

"You see, I lost my black cocker spaniel a few months ago, and I just want another to fill his place in my heart. I thought I'd try another breed, but I just can't get another picture in my head of the dog I want at the foot of my bed," the new owner told me.

Her cocker had died of old-age complications. Her heart was broken, and I could tell that she loved Manfred instantly. The love was mutual, because Manfred didn't even cast me a backward glance as he hopped into his new owner's car.

It always amazes me how God makes a comedy of errors work to bring all things to a good end. From dogs shooting out a front door, finding their way to a stranger who helped them, and then fulfilling a desire of a woman in another state who wanted just the dog I had—all things worked together for good.

Sometimes, as events happen through our day that get on our nerves and try our patience, maybe it's just God at work. Perhaps it is those very "patience zappers" that get us out of our comfort zone and force us to look outside our everyday box to find a bigger world of gifts elsewhere.

Perhaps Manfred's story began all because a woman in Indiana prayed for a black cocker spaniel.

The air of heaven is that which blows between a horse's ears.

—*ARABIAN PROVERB*

Maria's Wings

She was known simply as Mama Horse when I met her. A big black shining Tennessee Walking Horse, she was much nobler than her humble name. She was just part of the farm when it was bought, a fixture, like a faucet knob or a cattle gap on the property. I was just a guest invited out for a ride.

Every time I visited Shell Creek Farms in Eagleville, Tennessee, I got to ride Mama Horse. It had been years since I had ridden. My first horse was an ill-mannered old farm nag named Tony with a rickety stride of a gait, so when I climbed on Mama Horse and felt the smooth relaxed rocking motion of her beneath me, I fell in love. Her big brown eyes were ringed with white, a sign of fear and mistrust. My eyes were pretty much the same while I got to know her.

Our little affair started with apples, peppermints, and hours of brushing. Then I began taking on more and more responsibility where she was concerned. Her feet were trimmed up now, and she wore shoes instead of the accepted "pregnant barefoot" look of an old brood mare. I noticed something about Mama Horse when she hit the practice ring. She carried herself differently. Her gait stepped up. She had the heart of a show horse, and it was coming back to her. I guess if you were a retired professional in any field, the minute you felt yourself back in step with your memories, it would propel you into your past with great fervor. It certainly seemed to with Mama Horse. Her head bobbed, and her gait became even and shuffling almost as if she could remember the distant applause of celebrations past.

Mama Horse had an earth energy of healing that zoomed into me like a synergistic flash of power. I could throw my arms around her and quietly hold her, feeling her strength as it fed me. She generously shared as if it were her gift to me. I swear, if she could have she would have wrapped around me like a big velvet blanket. As we grew to be friends, her eyes softened. She forgave whoever had hurt her in her past, as did I, in a passage of affection between us. She was my healer, and I became hers. I loved her into loving me, which somehow made me more than I had been.

It wasn't long before I realized I could no longer just visit Mama Horse. She and I were meant to be together. So after paying the "take her off my hands" price of five hundred dollars, the old brood mare became my Maria. Her new name suited her regal personality.

I moved her to Hidden Acres Farm, a beautiful walking horse breeding and boarding farm on the Cumberland River. Her baby, Fancy, came along too. (That's another story.)

Maria became my joy, my prized possession, my center of gravity. Somewhere, our souls connected. From trail rides to just watching sunsets together in her stall, I depended on my Maria time. Her game of refusing to be caught was maddening at times, but never for long. For as you got just near enough to slip her halter on in the pasture, she'd flag her tail and snort as she'd narrowly escape with her neck arched and proud. It always somehow brought tears to my eyes. She was the total embodiment of freedom. Maria was old and a shadow of her regal past, but she never lost her spirit of youth. I made a mental note to carry my Maria spirit with me into my old age. It was a fiery joyous energy I loved about her.

Our sunsets were so special. I would quietly turn my back to her in her stall, and she'd rest her head on my shoulder. Our breathing would quietly even out into the same rhythm, and like hypnosis she'd lull away any angst of my day. I would always wait until there were no other boarders at the barn. Our time was too special to share. Few people ever knew we had such a faithful vigil.

Oh, a few people made fun of my senior citizen purchase. I just loved that when the group got lost on the trail, Maria was always the one who would quickly find her way back to the trailer when the word *home* was mentioned. She could move smoother and faster than other horses at a trot, while she never broke her well-bred running walk. Her veins pumped with the blood of champions, I know, even though there were no papers to prove it. She was my Sacajawea, leading us like pioneers to a safe place. Maria even brought applause by coming in third place in a barrel racing competition at the little fun show between boarders at the farm. She was just the fastest walker anyone had ever seen.

We didn't know how old Maria was. We just guessed. After Fancy, she bore Tucker, a little colt that looked just like her. Yes, he is another story, too. But the funny thing about Maria and babies: she always worked better alone than with our help. Though we tried, we weren't there to see her bring Tucker into this world. He was just a perfectly formed little surprise that she presented to us early one February morning. She was so proud. If I showed up, she'd nudge Tucker and make him get up and come to us for examination. "Look what I did," she seemed to say. "I'm really good at this." Like everything else, she certainly was.

Anyone could ride Maria. Her gentle way converted many a nonrider to a horse lover. On Christmas day, I'll never forget her giving my dad a ride. He'd happily say, "Hey, look, no hands! She knows exactly where she's going." Of course she did.

The kids came out from church one sunny Sunday afternoon and brushed and rode Maria as if she was the most incredible thing they'd ever experienced. She patiently let them walk around, under, and beside her without as much as a twinge of nervousness. She was such a mama. They loved her and thought she was the best horse in the whole world. And of course, she was.

She loved having babies and loved taking care of them. Her low, sweet nicker babied even the other horses in the barn. Other horses besides Fancy and Tucker came to her for motherly energy. Her boyfriend was Patch, a beautiful black-and-white gelding that had a thing for "his older woman." She spent most of her days watching the mares and foals at the farm. Unfortunately, her baby-producing days were over, according to the vet who had helped her with breedings past. This was a little depressing for my old girl. She had a bit of a sadness in her eyes as she watched the babies now.

Her coat still shone like black-blue fire, even in the dead of winter when other horses were shaggy and dull. She loved her new winter blanket that I fastened on at night. She loved to run and to get in the trailer to go anywhere and to be brushed. Oh, the hours of brushing and bonding we experienced!

Then one day, with no warning, things changed. My dear friend Alisa happened by the barn and called me in a panic. Maria was going down fast, and there was nothing we could do. With older animals, although you know the inevitable will happen, you are just never prepared for it when it does. And the next twenty-four hours were the most difficult of my life. She, like an Indian warrior, showed no signs of pain, even though her heart rate was at eighty-three (a horse's normal rate is around thirty-three). She didn't roll or bite or stomp her feet—not my girl. No, she just stood there looking at me with those aged, gentle eyes and quietly sent me the message, *It is my time, my friend.*

We did everything we could. The pain medication kept her from suffering. Then under the most beautiful, bright full moon I had ever seen, we walked to the pasture near the mare and baby paddock. Every horse in the barn nickered goodbye as she passed. They all knew. Then with the gentle hand of the vet, we watched her spirit rise from her body and ride into heaven like the sigh of a ship going down, her spirit too strong for her body to hold any longer.

After everyone had left, I lay by her body, still warm and silent. Our good-byes had been said as the sun had set that afternoon, just like so many afternoons before. I just had to touch her one more time, to feel the velvet of her nose as I kissed her, to wrap my arms around her neck just once more.

She was buried in the mare and baby paddock, because that was her favorite place.

I will never forget my precious old friend, who loved me and trusted me, and in so doing taught me to do the same. I can still smell her breath like fresh alfalfa on a spring day. I can still remember her queenly snort as she played "catch me if you can." I can still remember how her spirit felt as it flowed into me like great gulps of fresh air as I wrapped around her being with all I had. God, I will miss her.

Now on the banks of the Cumberland River, as the riverboats pass and the birds sing of sunset, is a paddock that I like to think is protected by the angel of my Maria, a paddock where she can always watch the babies play. And sometimes on the most beautiful of nights, when the moon is crystal clear and full, you can hear the low, sweet, gentle nicker of a Mama Horse named Maria. Of course, she will have wings.

Birthright

Somewhere in the Valley of Horses,
Spirits like ours are born.
We run with the blood of the ancients,
Coursing through us like a storm.

Never do we feel the anger
Of the fire called Mother Earth,
For she is the passion inside us,
And she breathed into us courage at birth.

We will fight the reins of all riders,
Choosing instead to be free
For we would rather die horses
Than anything less we could be.

—DEVON O'DAY

*Dogs act exactly the way we
would act, if we had no
shame.*

—CYNTHIA HEIMEL

Taz, the Wild Man

Helen at the Animal Control facility in Springfield, Tennessee, is an amazing woman. She is what in the "old days" we would have called a dogcatcher. But contrary to the image of the evil, foreboding little man with the great big net, Helen wears her uniform with a code of honor, decency, and humanity that I've never found before in an animal control officer.

She loves the animals that she has in the tiny shelter in Robertson County. She calls desperately trying to find homes for the dogs and cats that come to her there. She tries, but often does not succeed, and she must humanely do what she has been hired to do. Helen goes home with a broken heart on many nights.

One morning, she called me on the radio show about a golden retriever the fire department had surrendered. They had hoped to make him a "fire dog," but he just wasn't working out.

Of course, as soon as the radio show was over, I was on the first thing smoking to Springfield, and a half hour later I had Taz, the Wild Man, in the truck heading to the vet. We had to shave him down because of the mats in his hair, then he was checked out thoroughly and got his shots.

After a few days of ads and radio announcements, I placed Taz in a home. Dogs that have known many masters might take a little extra time in the "bonding" process. They know no strangers; however, a many-home adoptee may also know no friends.

Taz was not a full golden, or if he was, some puppy mill or backyard breeding was involved because he just wasn't built quite like any golden retriever I'd ever seen. He had a head shaped like a Great Dane. His legs were quite a bit longer than a golden. But in color and temperament he was definitely sweet and playful. The biggest problem with Taz was that he was a retrieving savant. He was like "Rain Man" when it came to retrieving. He's the only dog I have ever known that would rather retrieve than eat. If you threw a ball a million times into a driving rain, Taz would get it every time. He loves it. He lives for it. He was returned to me because of it.

Apparently the little boy in the family wanted a "buddy," and Taz was more interested in a ball-throwing machine. But as always in the placement of one of my animals, if you don't like them, call me. I'll come get them. So Taz boomeranged back to me.

I have tried over and over to place him, but the story is always the same. He is more interested in his ball than anyone who has him. So I guess Taz is mine for keeps. In fostering animals, you always take the chance on having to keep one that is unadoptable for some reason.

I often think that it is those animals that God has sent specifically to teach us something. In Taz's case I think that I have learned focus. In all the blur of life, it is very easy to forget our focus. We get consumed in the life going on around us and find ourselves caught up in someone else's dream. We get frustrated over not being able to achieve what someone else wants for his or her life. When in truth, all we really want for our joy may be to go "chase a ball."

We have all been given a ball to retrieve. We have a simple calling that has been given to us, and we have been given the gifts to accomplish that calling. It all comes from God. When we lose that focus on the gifts we've been given and the calling that God has made, we find ourselves awash in unhappiness and frustration.

Painters try to sing. Speakers try to be stockbrokers. Dancers become electricians, and the horror of life begins. Perhaps Taz has the right idea. He came to earth a retriever. It is his calling to bring things back. He does it, easily, and he is happy. In my life, I have things that I can do easily that I have shunned because they seemed easy. Nothing easy is worth having, right?

Wrong. If our natural abilities mean some things come easy for us, we should take advantage of them. God gives us the talent and has a plan; it's our job to focus on those things. When we discover our talents and learn to love ourselves for who we are, then we can truly be happy.

So now I'm going to throw Taz a ball and remind myself again to focus on what's important.

The Lord is My Shepherd

The Lord is my shepherd; I shall not want.
He makes me lie down in green pastures;
He leads me beside the still waters.
He restores my soul;
He leads me in the paths of righteousness for
    His name's sake.
Yea, though I walk through the valley of the
    shadow of death,
I will fear no evil; for You are with me;
Your rod and Your staff, they comfort me.
You prepare a table before me in the presence of
    my enemies;
You anoint my head with oil;
My cup runs over.
Surely goodness and mercy shall follow me
All the days of my life;
And I will dwell in the house of the Lord forever.

—PSALM 23

Show me your horse, and I will tell you who you are.

—ENGLISH PROVERB

Fancy's Dance

Shell Creek Stables was a beautiful storybook place in Eagleville, Tennessee, where a creek ran from a sunrise to a sunset and the valley was always a shade of golden amber. That was the place I first saw Fancy.

Her mother was my Maria, the first horse I ever bought. But Fancy won my heart the moment I saw her. Somewhere in my childhood dreams, I had seen her like a premonition of this moment: a young black and white filly with a fuzzy mane and delicate features. From dreamscape to reality—there she was before me. I guess, because she was such a part of my foreshadowing dreams, I recognized her and knew instantly she would be mine.

Everyone discouraged me about getting this unruly little creature. I called her Fancy because she looked as if she were wearing a fancy pair of pants across her hindquarters. She walked and did her round pen work (where horses are trained to walk, trot, and canter, and to use a rein, back pad, and then saddle) daintily. Tiny hooves moved in a 1-2-3-4 rhythm in a perfect saddle horse gait. Of course she had the awkward headset of a teenager, but I knew she'd grow into such a beauty.

Fancy was scared of her shadow, which led all the "horsey types" to *tsk-tsk* about "moonblindness," when a horse doesn't like daylight. Maybe she had moonblindness, or maybe she was just scared. Alisa helped me with her in basic training, but the truth between Fancy and me was created just between us two.

I whispered to her.

I am not a "horse whisperer," if there is such a thing. I just whispered commands to her. I wanted her to be able to hear me, to be calmed by me, and to learn that when I whispered to her, she could trust me. All the horse "know-it-alls" told me that to whisper was silly, and it would probably get me killed. Well, I'm still breathing, and it's uncanny how I can whisper across a pasture, and she'll look up from whatever she's doing and come to me. Maybe it's just a coincidence, but if it works, it certainly beats the run-around-the-field-with-arms-flying approach my fellow "experts" suggested.

It took almost a year to get Fancy to walk in a wash rack. It took most of that same year to get her into a trailer. But when a horse is afraid, it isn't being stubborn. I wasn't in a race to get her any of those places, so time and patience will always beat fear in the most wonderful peaceful of ways. I constantly loved her, praised her, and faced her fears with her. Every time I have ever felt her shake in fear, I have whispered softly like her mother's soft nicker in the night. Her shaking softens, her eyes are no longer rimmed in white, and she trusts. Fancy, like many show horses, is skittish and easily frightened; it's the way she is and always will be. I never mind reassuring her that her fear is real, but as long as I am with her, I will never lead her into anything that will hurt her. One foot at a time, we have moved through time into a place of horse and rider.

When I am on her back, Fancy "dances." She flitters from one side to the next, seeing scary objects along the trail. I have to be both alert and calming. She knows my fear, feels it, and will reflect it. Every movement in my mind goes directly into hers. It is much like the energy between people that goes unsaid, but not unfelt. Peace always comes back with a whispered "I'm here, girl. I won't ever do anything to hurt you. I won't ask anything of you that will put you in danger."

One foot, then the other, then two more follow, and we are home. I have blue ribbons hanging in the barn from shows that she's won for model classes, which I call "beauty pageants." She's probably never going to be a bombproof trail horse and an easy ride, but she was definitely supposed to be mine.

As I have taught her trust by being patient, slow, and kind, I have taught myself trust. Her fear is real, and so has mine been. As I whisper to her, "It's okay, girl . . . I've got you . . . just one foot in front of the other," I am also whispering those words to myself.

All of our fears are real. They may not be real for everybody, but for us they are reality. God says that He won't give us more than we can bear. Sometimes He sends us a helper, whether it be a person or an angel.

There is no fear in love . . .

—I JOHN 4:18

A Daisy Petal

For years I've dreamed of having a farm of my own. My grandfather's eighty acres in the swamps of Louisiana may not seem like much to ranchers in Texas or to the bluegrass bluebloods of Kentucky, but it was his Garden of Eden. That love of a little "spread in the country" was as bred into me as my height and eye color.

Of course, my farm is still a dream in the far distance as I push forty, but it doesn't mean I don't drive around country roads and imagine that one of the driveways I pass will one day be mine. On one of these country drives of imaginary estate ownership, I met Daisy.

I was driving around Ashland City, Tennessee, trying to get to the highway that would lead me back to Nashville. Instead of the road leading me southeast and back to town, I ended up going northwest toward Kentucky. Sense of direction was never part of my breeding, I guess. Getting lost often brings on a panic attack, and just as I began to get worried and my heart started to beat faster, I passed a Dalmatian on the side of the road. Just as I passed her, our eyes met, and I glanced in my rearview mirror to see her fall to the ground.

Suddenly, being lost was the least of my worries. I turned my truck around, and parked it close enough to walk toward her without frightening her.

As I got near, I noticed that the "collar" she was wearing was a boat chain that had literally grown into her neck. She had been hit by a car, or several of them, because she had a head injury and her back leg had been crushed and was hanging from her body. That is all I could survey from where I stood.

I thought of going to the area houses, which were sparse in that neck of the woods, to see if she belonged to anyone. However, after seeing her cruel makeshift collar, I decided no one who'd allow that to happen deserved her.

Approaching a hurt animal, especially as a stranger, is not something I recommend. It's simply not the smartest thing to do. But I knew this dog needed me and was in an emergency life or death moment. I took my chances.

"Old girl, you can trust me or not, but I think I might be your last chance," I slowly said in a low tone, moving toward her gently. I prayed she wouldn't take my hand off as I reached for her.

As I slid my hands under her malnourished body, she went limp in my arms. I carried her to my truck, feeling blood rush out of her leg and drip from her mouth.

"Please don't die, please don't die," I pleaded with her and God as I drove like a bat out of Carlsbad to find a vet in this town I was lost in. No one seemed to know where a vet clinic was. How could that be? I thought people in the country *had* animals. Obviously, they didn't use a vet to take care of them, if these people were any indication. Finally someone told me he thought one was next door to the Super Wal-Mart.

Well, a sense of a direction I don't have, but I have a radar that is foolproof for finding a Wal-Mart. And, yes, right next door to "the falling prices" was the Cheatham County Animal Hospital. They rushed the dog I was carrying into an exam room without pausing. She was in severe shock and had internal bleeding. Before X-rays or tests we had no idea what we were in for, or if she'd even last through the night.

"I'll pay for it, just please don't let her die," I begged them in desperation.

Looking back, they must have thought I was a nut, covered in blood from a dog I didn't know, saying I'd pay whatever it cost. Looking back, I'm thinking I must have been a nut. I didn't even ask what it would cost.

I called back every hour, until I could come sit with her just before closing.

The X-rays showed a totally destroyed leg that had to either come off or be reconstructed with metal and pins. I chose amputation, because I knew she'd probably heal better from that, and it was all I could afford.

Turns out, the vet team of husband and wife were from Louisiana too. We knew some of the same people. Then they realized they'd heard me on the radio doing animal charity events and pet placements, and helped me as best they could with the cost of everything. I guess at that point it was official—I was a nut, and they took pity on me.

Our girl made it through the night, and the next few days, and then amputation surgery like a champ. I went to see her twice a day, and she wagged her tail more each time she saw me. She was gaining her strength back, day by day.

Her collar had to be cut off and out with bolt cutters. Her head injuries left her with one pupil permanently dilated and a dent where her skull had been fractured. On the radio I told the tale of Daisy, named for the flower we used in the children's game of "he loves me, he loves me not"—because she had lost her leg, one of her "petals." Radio listeners and friends helped me pay for the cost of her care, which was well over a thousand dollars at that point.

Then almost three weeks later, Daisy was ready to go home. Home? Where was *that* going to be? I had a full quota of pets at my house, and I hadn't found a home with my listeners, or the pet hotline either. It was the rock and the hard place for us, Daisy and me. The only call I had gotten was from some goofy guy who sold roses out of a bucket on the interstate exit who thought he'd sell more from pity for a three-legged dog. Daisy was *not* going home with him!

My friend Alisa offered to foster Daisy until we found her a suitable home. An hour after she'd been delivered, I got the call that Daisy *was* at her suitable home. She stayed at Alisa's. It was Daisy's sweet brown eyes that won her new mom over.

A few months later, Daisy was in to get spayed when the vet called Alisa.

"You might be a little late for spaying," the vet told my friend. "She's already having puppies!"

"What?!" my friend asked.

Eleven pups later, everyone realized Daisy had been so malnourished and her health problems so great, no one had even thought about puppies. Daisy wasn't a full-blooded Dalmatian, but she was close enough in appearance to leave everyone thinking that eleven puppies might as well be a hundred and one. They were everywhere. Little black spotted babies filled her igloo in the backyard.

Daisy was an excellent mother, even without her one back leg. In fact, it probably made for easy access for all the babies to get to dinner without anything getting in the way.

When it came time to find homes for the babies, we went where I know you can always find anything you need. Wal-Mart! We needed homes for eleven puppies, and we found them in the Wal-Mart parking lot. Wal-Mart was sure coming in handy for Daisy.

We screened the new owners quickly, getting addresses and vet information. Most of the new families lived right in the neighborhood, and continue to use the same veterinarian as Daisy. Some of them even keep in touch.

Now, Daisy loves running sentry in her back yard, and stretching out in front of the fireplace at night with her two golden retriever housemates. She's the picture of healthy happiness, a long way from her start on that desolate roadside.

Looking back, I wonder if it was a wrong turn at all that day that brought me to Daisy. Perhaps, it was just a desperate cry from one of God's creatures into the universe, and He answered her prayer.

We cannot save every animal by every roadside. We can't always stop. We can't always get them into the car. We can't always get them to live through the night. But on this one occasion, this one dog lived to make a difference in my life, and to all the lives she has touched.

And to this day, every time I see a daisy, I am moved to pull off a petal, and whisper to myself with a smile, *she loves me.*

We have almost forgotten how strange a thing it is that so huge and powerful and intelligent an animal as a horse should allow another, and far more feeble animal, to ride upon its back.

—PETER GRAY

Tuckaboo's Farm

Tucker was never a rescue. Tucker was a planned pregnancy for my precious Maria, a Tennessee Walking Horse with a maternal energy second to none. We were at Hidden Acres Walking Horse Farm in Nashville, and Mr. Hoyte Eakes had a beautiful black-and-white stallion named Paints Impala. I knew from the first time I saw the graceful shuffle gait of that stallion that he and Maria would make a beautiful baby.

I was right, and on the cold morning of February 6, when the farmhands went to Maria's stall to feed her, a little colt poked his head out from underneath her. She was so proud; she'd taken care of everything all by herself. I called the colt beautiful because he was mine and because he came from Maria, but nothing could have been further from the truth.

So Tucker became his name. Maria would push Tucker over to me every time I walked in. Tucker would actually lie down across my lap, until he got too big. Then we switched places. I'd walk in during his naptime and sit on him. I'd rub his shoulders and scratch behind his ears. I didn't realize until much later that sitting on a sleeping horse isn't the safest thing to do, according to the horsey people who "know everything" there is to know about horses. I guess they didn't know Tucker and me very well. I never felt in danger, and the trust he had in me that allowed this made it easy to ride him later.

Tucker was more puppy than horse. He followed me around the pasture, as he did everyone. He was just lovesick for attention and horse "cookies" (actually horse treats called Whinny Treats). In showing him constant love and attention, I have always been able to get Tucker to do just about anything. He's never bucked or caused any problems. There's never been any kicking or biting.

I did, however, find that he knows how to jump a ravine, if he's scared and trying to get back to a barn!

Tucker is living proof that unconditional, constant, consistent love will move mountains. He's proof that you don't have to hurt something to make it do anything. He's proof that if you ask in kindness, you get kindness in return. Tucker is my proof that love and kindness work.

Author's Note: Tucker's mother died on his third birthday, the day I began this book, and a year later on that same date, the contract for this book was signed with Rutledge Hill Press.

For the animal shall not be measured by man. In a world older and more complete than ours they move finished, and complete . . . gifted with extensions of the senses we have lost, or never attained, living by voices we shall never hear.

—HENRY BESTON IN THE
OUTERMOST HOUSE

Pickles, Please

The dog pound is not the place any dog wants to end up. *Lady and the Tramp* was the first movie that horrified me by showing dogs in cages watching their days count down. Ever since I saw that movie, I can't give up the notion of stopping by, taking a look, and trying to "save" something.

I'm sure a therapist would have a heyday with my savior complex, but all codependence aside, it's just something I do. So far, saving animals has done more for me than any of the other vices I could fall back on, so I guess I'll take the lesser-of-two-evils approach.

In one of my pound visits, I came across an old golden retriever. I'm just a sucker for goldens to begin with, and this one stole my heart at first glance. Everyone heads to the puppy and kitten section at animal shelters. The cute factor is the big selling feature, and most people feel they can bond better with a younger animal. Nothing could be more untrue. Animals have unconditional bonding to someone—anyone—who loves them at any age. Old dogs *can* learn new tricks, and they make amazing pets for children.

Old dogs aren't bad about chewing, especially in Pickles' case. He was around fourteen and had almost no teeth. He was almost totally deaf, and couldn't see very well. His back legs shook from time to time, and his face was totally white with age. I knew this dog had belonged to someone. He had kindness in his eyes. His face pleaded, *I don't know how I got here, but please take me home.*

I went back every day for a week, and this old face kept haunting me. I watched the days get marked off on this kindly old gentleman's card, and on the last day I went back for him.

"Why would you want a dog that old?" the lady behind the counter asked me.

"Why wouldn't I?" was my response.

The door opened and the attendant was almost bowled over when Pickles came bounding out. There was a waiting room full of people, but he came directly to me. He didn't even sniff another person in the room. For a blind and deaf dog, I think this was a pretty remarkable accomplishment.

He had to be lifted into my Jeep but was right at home. He knew he was safe and happy and he was going to be loved.

Now Pickles runs with the other dogs at Big Sky Heaven Blue Farm where we live. He's slower than all the others. He has to have special, softer food. But every night when he stretches out on the rug in front of the fireplace in the most contented of sleeps, I am grateful he chose me.

There are old dogs and cats forgotten in shelters all across America. Each one was someone's pet that got lost, stolen, or separated from its family and couldn't find its way back. They are usually housetrained and loving and mild mannered with children. They are the old souls that cry out that there is still life to be lived and love to be given.

I can't help but see how God teaches us the lesson of the old forgotten ones through animals. There are elderly people filled with joy and wisdom of the ages forgotten in nursing homes and retirement centers everywhere. They watch the clock tick off minutes of precious life, just waiting for someone to stop by and give them a moment of conversation. They know so much. They have lived it. Yet they are just sitting in the hope that someone will stop and hold their hand, listen to an old repeated story, and brighten their day.

We all, as humans, have so many days on this earth. Like an old dog in a shelter, we mark them off one by one until we face the final one. I have learned from Pickles that it is not how many days you have left, but how you use each one that matters. He's taught me what it means to use those days—best.

Cats

There are no ordinary cats.
Time spent with cats is never wasted.
By associating with the cat, one only risks becoming richer.

I am indebted to the species of the cat for a particular kind of honorable deceit, for a great control over myself, for a characteristic aversion to brutal sounds, and for the need to keep silent for long periods of time. Our perfect companions never have fewer than four feet!

—COLETTE

*The cat has too much spirit
to have no heart.*

—ERNST MENAUL

Truck Stop BooBoo

My vet, Dr. McCormick, often called me when someone brought him a "foundling" to place. Sometimes it was just a
request to make a few phone calls to see if anyone had room for a
new pet. Other times, it was a plea of desperation. On this particular occasion, it seemed more the latter because he didn't hold out
much hope for the survival of the little kitten that had been left with
him that morning.

"I don't know if you'd even be interested in helping," he hedged.
"But this little guy was found on the tire of a big rig over at the
Cracker Barrel. He's only about four weeks old, and the driver who
found him said all his brothers and sisters had met their end right
there in the parking lot. As it looks, this kitten is the only one left,
and the trucker didn't have the heart to leave him."

"Is he weaned?" I asked.

"Well, I doubt it . . . so that means you'll probably have to feed him formula every couple of hours, keep him really warm, and even then . . . there's no guarantee he'll make it through. You might even be too busy to take this on, but I knew if anyone could nurse him through, it'd be you."

Of course I had to go take a look, and when I saw the kitten I was amazed at how small it was.

"How'd the trucker even see him? He's just so tiny," I wondered out loud.

"He was screamin' his head off, the trucker said." Dr McCormick told me. "He could even hear him over the highway noise. So I guess he really wanted to be found."

Well, the whole scenario appealed to my *I'll-save-you* complex, so of course I said yes. I bundled up the protesting bundle of feline fuzz, just big enough to fit in the palm of my hand. I drove down the street to my house and introduced "Boo" to Yogi, my golden retriever. Yogi has always had amazing familial instincts and instantly began nudging and grooming Boo while I concocted a baby formula.

I heated some evaporated milk and mixed it with some kitten replacement formula. I tested it on my forearm for temperature just like human baby formula, before I put it in Boo's little saucer. I had used a doll bottle to feed my first cat, Shaz, but I didn't have one handy. The weaning process for this cat was going to have to take place pretty quickly if he was going to survive.

I scooped him up off the floor and placed him on the counter by the saucer of warm formula. He wouldn't go near it. He just looked at it and screamed. Boo really was like an infant throwing a tantrum. His tail stood straight up in the air. He wouldn't even try to taste the food before him. So thinking of what mother cats do, I picked Boo up by the scruff of the neck. He "froze" at my touch, and I had instant control of my new baby.

I physically stuck his small muzzle into the warm liquid until he had a milk beard. The tongue went out, his belly responded, and he splashed body and all into the saucer. He began licking the milk off his fur. It took several "lessons" before he realized he didn't have to bathe with his food to eat it. I set my clock and got up several times to feed him.

I made a miniature litter box, so he would have no trouble climbing in. I'd place Boo in the box, then scratch a dune or two across the litter with his front paw. He didn't get the idea right away, but after I rubbed the area where his tail joined his back, he moved into position. And *voila!* I have never been so overjoyed at cat toiletry than at that moment. When he finished, I showed him how to cover "his spot" with his front paws.

Next I imitated a mother cat by cleaning him all over with a hot wet washcloth wrung dry. The rough nap of the cloth against him was like the rough tongue of his mother. He curled up on my chest and went to sleep.

Sometime during the night, Boo made his way to the curve of my golden retriever's belly and made himself at home. For the remainder of his time with me, Boo slept curled against Yogi, making "biscuits" against him as kittens do with their mothers during feeding. Yogi loved Boo and carried him gently from room to room in his mouth. There was never a time I could pick up Boo that he wasn't wet or a little stiff from dog spit. He had a serious case of Mohawk punk-do going on when that stuff dried.

The liquid diet quickly moved to kitten chow soaked in the formula, then to chow in warm water, then chow next to water. At eight weeks old, Boo was fully functional and a true survivor, still screaming for attention and anything he wanted. No doubt how he made it this far: lung power!

Now was the hard part of being a foster parent—finding the perfect home. It's hard to let go of an animal you've taught to live. You do get attached. You do fall in love. You do miss them when they are gone. Most people think that foster animal homes are manned by people who've gotten used to saying goodbye, and that it somehow gets easier because we do it so much. That will never be the case. Every animal I love is part of me when I say goodbye. It will never grow easy, but it will always be . . . my job.

I went to the radio station to do a little work over the weekend, and I found Bama, one of our weekend announcers on the air. I don't know how it came up, but I mentioned Boo, his story, and the need for an amazing home for him.

It was as if the heavens opened and the angels started singing, because Bama lit up like a Christmas tree.

"I have to see him! I want a playmate for my old cat, Hobbs. This little guy sounds perfect!" Bama exclaimed.

Twenty-four hours later, the kitten was getting socialized to an old cat at Bama's apartment. I have never known a man to love cats as much as Bama. He has spoiled them rotten, and still calls me often to tell me of Boo and Hobbs' shenanigans. He's given me wonderful pictures and kept me abreast of every development. It seems old Hobbs has found his youth in the young friend who now shares his home.

I'm sure that truck driver seldom, if ever, thinks about the random act of kindness he performed and the ripple effect it had. Maybe we all create ripple effects we aren't aware of when we do something kind for an animal in need. I bet that trucker doesn't know that, because he cared enough to "waste" a little time, an old cat he's never seen has been given a friend to play with. He probably will never know how happy he's made a single guy who lives for the cats that welcome him home every night. I'm sure he won't ever know what a gift he gave me. I learned that "lost cases" are never lost for long . . . if they are given love, nurturing, and time. I guess that lesson is best practiced every time we look in a mirror.

Born to Be Happy

Freedom tastes a little bit like glory . . .
Don't think I'll ever touch the ground.
My song, might be everybody's story . . .
But maybe we've all got the need,
Maybe we're all born to be . . .
Happy.

—KIM PATTON-JOHNSTON

Horses lend us the wings we lack.

—*Pam Brown*

Poshee's Tale

When I was in grade school, I became fascinated with the Walter Farley books about horses. I read everything I could about horses of every kind. The Black Stallion, the King of the Wind, and Secretariat were the pinups I had on my wall. Sham, the Arabian stallion in *King of the Wind,* probably left the most indelible mark on my soul. His story made me dream of one day having an Arabian horse, with a finely chiseled neck arched in a graceful ballet of equine form. I yearned to feel the spirit and power of a horse bred to endure the desert sands, yet bearing beauty befitting royalty. I thought about that—a lot.

Sham was born with a little white spot on his back foot, just above the hoof. Legend said that any horse born with that little white spot was "kissed by the wind" and would be the fastest of the fast, or "the King of the Wind." Years later, one of the thoroughbreds that came in second to Secretariat in the Kentucky Derby and Preakness was also named Sham, which let me know I wasn't the only one who'd become fascinated with those stories.

I tell you all this because you must know this part of the story to understand the passion I felt for Poshee. I did not buy my own horse until I was thirty-five. I had ridden, yes, but I was by no means a rider. I learned how to post to the trot of a horse by reading a book. That should let you know how amazing I was on horseback—not!

I had two horses, both Tennessee Walking Horses, a breed I'm most connected to. At the boarding barn where I kept them was a horse that caught my eye, Poshee. He was a registered Arabian gelding, about 15.3 hands and thirteen years old. He'd been a stallion until he was eleven, which explained the spirit that he still maintained, quite well! No one explained to him the meaning of the word *gelded;* consequently he still acted like "king of the herd" around the barn.

I always considered a white horse to be a horse that was white. However, in the horse world, it was explained to me, what I thought was a white horse was a gray one. Grays have black skin underneath their hair and dark eyes. As they get older, grays get lighter, until they get little red flecks in their coat and become what is referred to as "flea-tick" or "flea-bit." I just hate that term, so I've always said that Posh was "white with freckles." It may not have been acceptable to the horse snobs who seemed to know everything, but it sounded much more lovable and romantic than "flea-tick"!

Our little "love affair" began slowly, when Posh began softly nickering to me when I fed my horses "cookies" at sundown each day. He always had the softest, sweetest voice if he thought there was something good to eat in the deal, and was filled with such love. Boarding barns are notorious gossip mills, especially with a lot of women about, and the gossip about Poshee's owner started running rampant. There were unkind rumors and judgments about how she wasn't paying

Poshee's bills and that his feet weren't being cared for, and a host of other gossip that really bothered me. I've never liked people making judgments, for one thing, but I certainly didn't want a horse to go without, either. I guess what chafed me most was that people could use words in such hurtful ways, never caring how deeply they cut.

"You should just buy Poshee, since the owner doesn't care about him," snapped a busybody boarder.

"Well, I just might," I answered, mulling over what I'd do with yet another horse to feed.

His owner's number was in the barn book, so I called her. Cynthia was her name, and I made her a much under-value offer to buy her horse. I had never met her, nor she me, so her answer was a quick and rather cold, snappy, "No!"

Weeks passed, and I ran into Cynthia at the barn, as Poshee was getting his "pedicure." That was the way I like to refer to getting shod. He was so delicate as he was getting worked on. His tiny black feet, characteristic of Arabians, gently stayed put on the tiny platform as Dave the blacksmith worked. I looked at Poshee, then at Cynthia his owner, and I discovered something about both of them. They really loved each other!

I also saw something in Cynthia's eyes that I recognized. I had looked out of eyes just like hers before. She was in an abusive or hurtful relationship, and it showed. Suddenly the pain in her heart leapt from hers into mine, and I understood everything so clearly.

"Can I talk to you?" I asked Cynthia.

"Okay," she answered as we walked out of the barn and stood looking at the sunset along the Cumberland River, which ran by the farm.

"I don't mean to pry, but is there something wrong?" I gently tried to broach an awkward subject.

Somehow, the cork was loosed and the words began to flow as

Cynthia explained how incredibly tough the last years had been. Health problems that had left her permanently disabled, the birth of a new son, and a husband who left upon spending all of her disability money just began the story. As the story unfolded I was in tears just as she was. She had never neglected Poshee! In fact, she gave him all she had to give. Cynthia had been doing the best she could.

Poshee had been hers from his birth, and she'd trained him herself. They'd competed in dressage together. She'd campaigned him and promoted his stallion career. He was her baby. They'd surely gone through a lot together. He had been born in Florida, next to an orange grove.

"He just loves navel oranges," she smiled, with a glisten of tears in her eyes. "They'd fall on the ground over the fence from the grove, and he'd eat them, peel and all, making these big sucking sounds. He's not much on apples, but just surprise him with an orange and see how he reacts!"

"Cynthia, you don't know me from Adam . . . but I'd like to make you an offer." I carefully thought out loud. "If you will let me, I'll pay you fifteen hundred dollars for Poshee. If at any time, you want to buy him back, you can, for the same amount of money. I promise never to sell him to anyone or to try and make a profit on him. I promise to love him as if he were mine. I promise always to give him a good home."

"Well, he's worth a lot more than that! He jumps; he is a great show horse; he's . . . my baby! You could sell him for at least twice that tomorrow!" she answered emotionally.

"I don't doubt any of that. But I'm giving you my word—I won't." I replied.

She went home to think about the proposition, and my phone rang the next day. Cynthia accepted my offer, and I paid her.

"Why are you doing this?" she asked me.

"Because I've looked through your eyes." I gave her an answer that needed no explanation. She immediately understood.

Cynthia sold her house and moved back to Florida with her toddler son to live with her mother. Posh and I still get a Christmas card each year from Cynthia. Her life has turned around in a beautiful way, as lives have a way of doing when you surrender all you cannot handle to a Higher Power that has a bigger dream for us than we do for ourselves. Her son is a wonderful confirmation that the "baby" who needed her most was in her arms.

And, now, so many years after reading about the regal speed, spirit, and agility of Sham, and yearning all my life for an Arabian horse of my own, I finally have one. We've been in the show ring. We've been trail riding in the Smoky Mountains. We've shared many a "cookie" at sunset.

However, the healing that Poshee has brought into my life has nothing to do with riding him. Every single time I lead him from his stall to the back pasture for the night, the picture is the same. I put my arms around his neck, feeling his pulse quicken, because he knows his "herd" is waiting. I kiss the soft velvet of his nose, breathing his horsey breath with the faint hint of orange. Then as I release him from his halter, he takes off with a puff of dust underneath him. Halfway back to the herd, he rises into the air on his back feet and paws powerfully with his front ones. He screams a mighty stallion scream that says, *I am here, now! You are all safe!*

Then as he runs as fast as he can, with his tail flagging in the wind, and his mane tossed wildly about his silhouette, I get tears in my eyes.

That is what freedom truly looks like. I am reminded each time that the greatest joy I will ever get from having Poshee is letting him go.

Dogs are our link to paradise.
They don't know evil, or jeal-
ousy, or discontent. To sit with
a dog on a hillside on a glorious
afternoon is to be back in Eden,
where doing nothing was not
boring, it was peace.

—MILAN KUNDERA

Dodi's Dream

One of the many hurt or lost animals brought to my
door by the Boxer of Mercy was a fat and waddling cocker spaniel I
named Dodi. She was at my front door one blustery, wet night, covered in mats of fur and shivering with cold.

Her sweetness was obvious as she walked in, and she didn't mind
at all when I put her in the tub of warm water and scrubbed her
clean. She was totally peaceful as I clipped the mats from her ears. I
think she lost ten pounds after the shearing.

Dodi must have belonged to someone, but she'd either been lost
for quite some time, or someone didn't care enough to keep her
clean or cared for. The tough part of animal rescue is knowing when
neglect is evident or when a dog is simply lost and trying to find its
way home.

The next day I listed Dodi in the lost and found. The ad ran a
week, and no one called. During the week, Dodi slept beside me, and

I realized she was the cuddliest of critters. If she didn't belong to someone, I'd be very surprised.

Most people assume when they find an animal that seems neglected that the culprit is a bad or cruel owner. That's not always the case. Sometimes people steal a dog and ask for a reward for "finding" a beloved pet. Dogs sometimes run off during storms and get disoriented and cannot find their way home. Sometimes a kind stranger will pick them up as strays, take them to a part of town totally foreign to the dog, and the dog escapes to try to get back home.

There are so many scenarios on the whys and hows of lost pets. Microchipping has helped, but it's no use after the fact. In Dodi's case, she had on a collar with no tag. No one answered the lost pet ad, so I had to assume Dodi was adoptable.

It only took a day to find her a home. "I'm Dodi, I'm an old black-and-white cocker, I'm clean and I'm housetrained and I love to be cuddled." The ad got so many calls that I just took the first one. An older couple adopted her and the next week called to say she was the best dog they'd ever had.

I'm often asked how I can give up adorable animals like Dodi. It's never easy, and there is always a catch in my heart as I say goodbye. But every happy adoption means one less unhappy animal in the world.

I've heard it said of shelters, "Oh, I could just take them all home!" No, you couldn't, if you want them to be healthy and happy. The most important part of what any person should consider about the fostering and adoption of animals is the compassion for the animal you adopt.

The greatest love is knowing what's best for those you love, and giving them that. God has given us amazing blueprints to show us how to love. First Corinthians 13, the "love chapter," explains it eloquently. But often we as humans don't get it. We stay in relationships out of obsession, jealousy, pride, and apathy. We forget to love ourselves, and we forget what loving another person looks like and feels like when it is good and holy and pure.

As Dodi waddled to her new owners, who instantly began cuddling and cooing over her, leaving her tootsie roll of a tail wagging to beat the band, I was reminded of pure love. It's opening your hands and letting go. It's giving away what you want for yourself. It's a warm feeling of joy that only comes from doing the right thing.

Dodi turned to me, in kind of a canine *thank you,* and then walked heart first, right into the arms of love. I hope that picture and how that moment felt live in my soul forever.

My little dog . . . a heartbeat at my feet.

—EDITH WHARTON

Henry's Hidden Heart

In a pen in the back of Nashville Humane Society was a growling mass of miniature black schnauzer. His back was laced together in stitches and drainage tubes, making him a bit of a Frankenstein mutt. On his pen was a sign that read: "AGGRESSIVE! BITES! UNADOPTABLE!"

Cherry, one of the volunteers at the Humane Association, had called me because I was on the schnauzer rescue list. She warned me he was not like any schnauzer she'd ever known, and even I might have second thoughts about him. Of course, when I met this angry little old man of fur, I had second, third, and fourth thoughts—all of which led me to take him home. His name became Henry, almost instantly. He just looked like a Henry.

He snapped when you touched him. He growled when you got near him. He snarled at his food. Basically, Henry was in a terminal case of "bad mood." I have known many people just like Henry.

They spend their entire days complaining and grumbling.

It didn't take long for Henry to become an escape artist. He would dig out of the fence and run to the front door and scratch to be let in. It was just his little game of saying, "I got out again . . . and you can't stop me!"

Henry hated everything. He hated all the other dogs. He hated the cats. He hated any human being who got near me. I still love the picture of my dear friend Hoss, who stopped by for a visit wearing what looked like a fluorescent tie-dyed caftan. It horrified Henry, who promptly chased him up on an ottoman, snarling and barking to keep this colorful boogeyman at bay. I honestly can't say that I liked Hoss' caftan, either, so I couldn't much blame Henry for that one.

My roommate at the time, Kris, would call to Henry as she stood at the front door, in her loudest Julia Child-Ethel Merman imitation. This was a sound that my parrot, Bernice, took to heart and continued constantly. Bernice's uncanny recounting of the "Henry call" was so lifelike that Henry was forever being tormented into coming into the parrot room, only to find no one. Bernice would call, he'd come running . . . and both would look bewildered at each other as if to say, "What?!"

Since he'd become such an escape artist—most schnauzers are—I put a red heart on his collar that said, "I'm Henry. I belong to Devon. If you find me, I'm lost. Please call her." I got calls from apartment complexes, neighbors down the street, and even one from the Cracker Barrel. Before you get upset and assume that I let my dogs run wild, you must realize that a six-foot privacy fence with cement blocks all around the edges still couldn't hold Henry. He had super-strength at digging and could move heavy items twice his size, if it meant freedom.

People have called and said, "Henry's here, and I think he's ready to go home." He'd make himself at home in each stranger's home until I got there. Then when I knocked on the door, he'd grumble as he trotted past me and got in the car. It was as if he were saying, "I know, I know, I meant to get lost. Let's just go home."

People always had a love-hate relationship with Henry. He was so cute, but always acted like he would take your hand off. He would take on a rottweiler without a fear in the world. He could dig to China and be covered in a beard full of dirt balls. He got skunked on a regular basis and was always being dumped in a tub to remove stinkiness of some kind.

With all the grumbling, the digging, the running away, and the personality of a wet granny, what was it about Henry that stole my heart? His spirit was as big as Montana, for one thing. There was never a door that could keep Henry from me. He would cock his ear and turn his head inquisitively to one side and stare at me intently, just waiting for a show of attention.

Henry, who grumbled the most, was the most affectionate dog I have ever had. He always had to be touching me. I could lie down for a quick nap, and Henry would circle in a spot against my back and curl in a ball of sleep as close as he could get. When I picked him up from the kennel, Henry would always be the first out, ready to sail into my arms.

He was patient during my meal times, knowing that if he lay quietly, he'd get a treat at the end of it. Henry has always had a way of reading my soul. Turns out, a lot of his apparent grumbling was him trying his best to communicate. His moans, growls, and whines were his words.

Henry has never done anything spectacular. He can't shake hands, do stupid pet tricks, or even manage to stay clean for more than an hour. But what Henry brought to my life was a sense of what the cover of a book can hide. Sometimes, the ones who gripe the loudest, and resist touch the most, are the ones with hidden hearts screaming out for love and affection. Henry has taught me not to judge someone with a loud voice and a crabby temperament so harshly. Sometimes those are the people who respond and crumble into a soft heap when they are approached in love.

Henry's scars still show when he's groomed in his summer short *schnauzer-do*. They stand as a reminder of a little dog with a great big spirit that fought for his honor with all the force he could muster and lived to tell about it. It is that kind of bravery that Henry has given me, to face my enemies and fears when they seem too big or too mean. Sometimes, the best reward for the hardest fight is finding a warm place to curl up next to someone who loves you—in spite of your growls and snarls. That, my friend, is love. Never settle for anything short of someone who adores your hidden heart.

ABOUT THE AUTHOR

Devon O'Day, with more than two decades in the business of "talking for a living," has always managed to find a way to use the airwaves as a platform for animal protection, placement, and promotion. She spends weekday mornings at the production helm for top morning radio host Gerry House at WSIX-FM and weekends hosting *Country Hitmakers,* a nationally syndicated country music audio magazine. You can hear her voice touting products such as Drexel Heritage Furniture, announcing at the Dove Awards, or narrating specials on The Learning Channel and Oster Pet Care videos.

As a songwriter, Devon has had songs recorded by George Strait, Hank Williams Jr., Marty Raybon, and LeeAnne Womack, to name a few. She will be quick to tell you that the best inspiration for many of her love songs has been the love she has celebrated in the animals that have graced her life.

With speaking engagements, horse shows, and charity events a big part of her life, Devon still gravitates to home in the lovely hills of Kingston Springs, Tennessee, just outside Nashville. Big Sky Heaven Blue Farm is filled with family, lots of furry friends, and a welcome mat for those that God sends its way.